Summer LINK
READING

McGraw Hill **Children's Publishing**

Columbus, Ohio

 Children's Publishing

Copyright © 2004 McGraw-Hill Children's Publishing. Published by American Education Publishing, an imprint of McGraw-Hill Children's Publishing, a Division of The McGraw-Hill Companies.

Send all inquiries to:
McGraw-Hill Children's Publishing
8787 Orion Place
Columbus, OH 43240-4027

ISBN 0-7696-3322-6

1 2 3 4 5 6 7 8 9 10 QPD 09 08 07 06 05 04

The McGraw-Hill Companies

Table of Contents

Summer Link Recommended Reading

- **Animal Close-Ups Series** — Barbara Taylor
- **Araminta's Paint Box; Song and Dance Man** — Karen Ackerman
- **The Arctic; The Desert; The Ocean; The Rain Forest** — Alan Baker
- **Eleanor, Ellatony, Ellencake, and Me!** — C.M. Rubin
- **Bird Watch: A book of Poetry** — Jane Yolen
- **Chester's Way; Julius, the Baby of the World** — Kevin Henkes
- **Chickens Aren't the Only Ones** — Ruth Heller
- **Dandelions; Fly Away Home** — Eve Bunting
- **Fox In Love** (first readers) — Edward Marshall
- **Good Driving, Amelia Bedelia** — Herman Parish
- **The Great Kapok Tree** — Lynne Cherry
- **Henry and Mudge Series** (first readers) — Cynthia Rylant
- **Ira Says Goodbye** — Bernard Waber
- **Little Critter Series** (first readers) — Mercer Mayer
- **Miss Rumphius** — Barbara Cooney
- **Molly and Emmett's Camping Adventure; Molly and Emmett's Surprise Garden** — Marylin Hafner
- **The Napping House** — Audrey and Don Wood
- **Noisy Nora** — Rosemary Wells
- **The Ox-Cart Man** — Donald Hall
- **Why Mosquitos Buzz in People's Ears** — Verna Aardema
- **Wolves** — R.D. Lawrence

Consonant Teams

Consonant teams are two or three consonant letters that have a single sound.
Examples: sh and **tch**

Directions: Write each word from the word box next to its picture. Underline the consonant team in each word. Circle the consonant team in each word in the box.

bench	match	shoe	thimble
shell	brush	peach	watch
whale	teeth	chair	wheel

Consonant Teams

Directions: Circle the consonant teams in each word in the word box. Write a word from the word box to finish each sentence. Circle the consonant teams in your words.

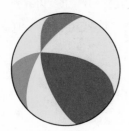

trash	splash	chain
shut	chicken	catch
ship	when	patch
	which	

1. My _____ won't lay eggs.

2. I put a _____ on my bicycle so nobody can take it.

3. We watched the big _____ dock and let off its passengers.

4. It is my job to take out the _____ .

5. I have to wear a _____ over my eye until it is better.

6. The baby likes to _____ in the bathtub.

7. Can you _____ the ball with one hand?

8. Please _____ the windows before it rains.

9. _____ are we going to leave for school?

10. I don't know _____ of these books is mine.

Name _____

Double Vowel Words

Usually when two vowels appear together, the first one says its name and the second one is silent.

Example: b<u>e</u>an

Directions: Unscramble the double vowel words below. Write the correct word on the line.

ocat _____

etar _____

mtea _____

eetf _____

teas _____

otab _____

ogat _____

spea _____

atli _____

apil _____

7

Name _____

Silent Letters

Some words have letters you can not hear at all, such as the **gh** in **night**, the **w** in **wrong**, the **l** in **walk**, the **k** in **knee**, the **b** in **climb**, and the **t** in **listen**.

Directions: Look at the words in the word box. Write the word under its picture. Underline the silent letters.

knife	light	calf	wrench	lamb	eight
wrist	whistle	comb	thumb	knob	knee

_____   _____   _____   _____

_____   _____   _____   _____

_____   _____   _____   _____

Review

Directions: Read the story. Circle the consonant teams (two or three letters) and silent letters in the underlined words. Be sure to check for more than one team in a word! One has been done for you.

One day last (spring), my family went on a picnic. My father picked out a <u>pretty spot</u> next to a <u>stream.</u> <u>While</u> my <u>brother</u> and I <u>climbed</u> a <u>tree</u>, my mother <u>spread</u> out a <u>sheet</u> and <u>placed</u> the food on it. But before we could eat, a <u>skunk</u> <u>walked</u> out of the woods! Mother <u>screamed</u> and <u>scared</u> the skunk. It <u>sprayed</u> us with a terrible <u>smell!</u> Now, we <u>think</u> it is a funny <u>story</u>. But <u>that</u> day, we ran!

Directions: Write the words with three-letter blends on the lines.

_____ _____ _____

_____ _____

Name _____

Review

Directions: Look through a magazine. Cut out pictures of nouns and glue them below. Write the name of the noun next to the picture.

Plurals

Plurals are words that mean more than one. You usually add an **s** or **es** to the word. In some words ending in **y**, the **y** changes to an **i** before adding **es**. For example, **baby** changes to **babies**.

Directions: Look at the following lists of plural words. Write the word that means one next to it. The first one has been done for you.

foxes	**fox**	balls	_____
bushes	_____	candies	_____
dresses	_____	wishes	_____
chairs	_____	boxes	_____
shoes	_____	ladies	_____
stories	_____	bunnies	_____
puppies	_____	desks	_____
matches	_____	dishes	_____
cars	_____	pencils	_____
glasses	_____	trucks	_____

Compound Subjects

Two similar sentences can be joined into one sentence if the predicate is the same. A **compound subject** is made up of two subjects joined together by the word **and**.

Example: Jamie can sing.
    Sandy can sing.

<u>Jamie **and** Sandy</u> can sing.

Directions: Combine the sentences. Write the new sentence on the line.

1. The cats are my pets.
   The dogs are my pets.

_____

2. Chairs are in the store.
   Tables are in the store.

_____

3. Tom can ride a bike.
   Jack can ride a bike.

_____

Verbs

Directions: Write each verb in the correct column.

| rake | talked | look | hopped | skip |
| cooked | fished | call | clean | sewed |

Yesterday

_____

_____

_____

_____

_____

Today

_____

_____

_____

_____

_____

Name _____

Compound Subjects and Predicates

The following sentences have either a **compound subject** or a **compound predicate**.

Directions: If the sentence has a compound subject (more than one thing doing the action), **underline** the subject. If it has a compound predicate (more than one action), **circle** the predicate.

Example: <u>Bats and owls</u> like the night.

The fox (slinks and spies.)

1. Raccoons and mice steal food.

2. Monkeys and birds sleep in trees.

3. Elephants wash and play in the river.

4. Bears eat honey and scratch trees.

5. Owls hoot and hunt.

Ownership

Directions: Read the sentences. Choose the correct word and write it in the sentences below.

1. The _____ lunchbox is broken.   boys   boy's

2. The _____ played in the cage.   gerbil's   gerbils

3. _____ hair is brown.   Anns   Ann's

4. The _____ ran in the field.   horse's   horses

5. My _____ coat is torn.   sister's   sisters

6. The _____ fur is brown.   cats   cat's

7. Three _____ flew past our window.   birds   bird's

8. The _____ paws are muddy.   dogs   dog's

9. The _____ neck is long.   giraffes   giraffe's

10. The _____ are big and powerful.   lion's   lions

Synonyms

Directions: Read each sentence. Fill in the blanks with the synonyms.

friend	tired	story
presents		little

I want to go to bed because I am very <u>sleepy</u>.

_____

On my birthday I like to open my <u>gifts</u>.

_____

My <u>pal</u> and I like to play together.

_____

My favorite <u>tale</u> is Cinderella.

_____

The mouse was so <u>tiny</u> that it was hard to catch him.

_____

Antonyms

Antonyms are words that are opposites.

Directions: Read the words next to the pictures. Draw a line to the antonyms.

dark   empty

hairy   dry

closed   happy

dirty   bald

sad   clean

full   light

wet   open

Antonyms: Completing a Story

Directions: Write opposite words in the blanks to complete the story.

hot	hard	top	cold	bottom
soft	quickly	happy	slowly	sad

One day, Grandma came for a visit. She gave my sister Jenny and me a box of chocolate candy. We said, "Thank you!" Then Jenny _____ took the _____ off the box. The pieces all looked the same! I couldn't tell which pieces were _____ inside and which were _____ ! I only liked the _____ ones. Jenny didn't care. She was _____ to get any kind of candy!

I _____ looked at all the pieces. I didn't know which one to pick. Just then Dad called us. Grandma was going home. He wanted us to say good-bye to her. I hurried to the front door where they were standing. Jenny came a minute later.

I told Grandma I hoped I would see her soon. I always feel _____ when she leaves. Jenny stood behind me and didn't say anything. After Grandma went home, I found out why. Jenny had most of our candy in her mouth! Only a few pieces were left in the _____ of the box! Then I was _____ ! That Jenny!

Homophones

Directions: Read each word. Circle the picture that goes with the word.

1. sun

2. ate

3. buy

4. hi

5. four

6. hear

Is, Are, and Am

Is, **are**, and **am** are special action words that tell us something is happening now.

Use **am** with **I**. **Example: I am**.
Use **is** to tell about one person or thing. **Example: He is**.
Use **are** to tell about more than one. **Example: We are**.
Use **are** with **you**. **Example: You are**.

Directions: Write **is**, **are**, or **am** in the sentences below.

1. My friends _____ helping me build a tree house.

2. It _____ in my backyard.

3. We _____ using hammers, wood, and nails.

4. It _____ a very hard job.

5. I _____ lucky to have good friends.

Was and Were

Was and **were** tell us about something that already happened.

Use **was** to tell about one person or thing. **Example:** I **was**, he **was**. Use **were** to tell about more than one person or thing or when using the word you. **Example:** We **were**, you **were**.

Directions: Write **was** or **were** in each sentence.

1. Lily _____ eight years old on her birthday.

2. Tim and Steve _____ happy to be at the party.

3. Megan _____ too shy to sing "Happy Birthday."

4. Ben _____ sorry he dropped his cake.

5. All of the children _____ happy to be invited.

Go, Going, and Went

We use **go** or **going** to tell about now or later. Sometimes we use **going** with the words **am** or **are**. We use **went** to tell about something that already happened.

Directions: Write **go**, **going**, or **went** in the sentences below.

1. Today, I will _____ to the store.

2. Yesterday, we _____ shopping.

3. I am _____ to take Muffy to the vet.

4. Jan and Steve _____ to the party.

5. They are _____ to have a good day.

Have, Has, and Had

We use **have** and **has** to tell about now. We use **had** to tell about something that already happened.

Directions: Write **has**, **have**, or **had** in the sentences below.

1. We _____ three cats at home.

2. Ginger _____ brown fur.

3. Bucky and Charlie _____ gray fur.

4. My friend Tom _____ one cat, but he died.

5. Tom _____ a new cat now.

See, Saw, and Sees

We use **see** or **sees** to tell about now. We use **saw** to tell about something that already happened.

Directions: Write **see**, **sees**, or **saw** in the sentences below.

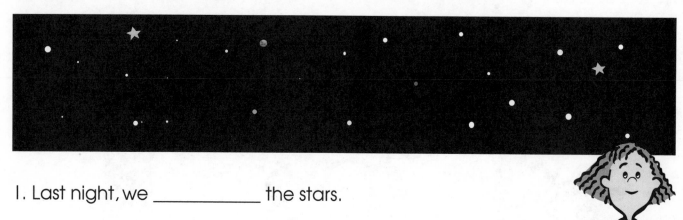

1. Last night, we _____ the stars.

2. John can _____ the stars from his window.

3. He _____ them every night.

4. Last week, he _____ the Big Dipper.

5. Can you _____ it in the night sky, too?

6. If you _____ it, you would remember it!

7. John _____ it often now.

8. How often do you _____ it?

Name _____

Eat, Eats, and Ate

We use **eat** or **eats** to tell about now. We use **ate** to tell about what already happened.

Directions: Write **eat**, **eats**, or **ate** in the sentences below.

1. We like to _____ in the lunchroom.

2. Today, my teacher will _____ in a different room.

3. She _____ with the other teachers.

4. Yesterday, we _____ pizza, pears, and peas.

5. Today, we will _____ turkey and potatoes.

Leave, Leaves, and Left

We use **leave** and **leaves** to tell about now. We use **left** to tell about what already happened.

Directions: Write **leave**, **leaves**, or **left** in the sentences below.

1. Last winter, we _____ seeds in the bird feeder everyday.

2. My mother likes to _____ food out for the squirrels.

3. When it rains, she _____ bread for the birds.

4. Yesterday, she _____ popcorn for the birds.

Sentences

Directions: Write capital letters where they should appear in the sentences below.

Example: joe can play in january.

1. we celebrate thanksgiving on the third thursday in november.

_____

_____

2. in june, michelle and mark will go camping every friday.

_____

_____

3. on mondays in october, i will take piano lessons.

_____

_____

Name _____

Parts of a Sentence

Directions: Look at the pictures. Draw a line from the naming part of the sentence to the action part to complete the sentence.

The boy   delivered the mail.

A small dog   threw a football.

The mailman   fell down.

The goalie   chased the ball.

Complete the Sentences

Directions: Write your own endings to make the sentences tell a complete idea.

Example:

The Wizard of Oz is a story about   <u>Dorothy and her dog, Toto</u> .

1. Dorothy and Toto live on _____.

2. A big storm _____.

3. Dorothy and Toto are carried off to _____.

4. Dorothy meets _____.

5. Dorothy, Toto, and their friends follow the _____.

6. Dorothy tries to find _____.

7. The Wizard turns out to be _____.

8. A scary person in the story is _____.

9. The wicked witch is killed by _____.

10. The hot air balloon leaves without _____.

11. Dorothy uses her magic shoes to _____.

Statements and Questions

Statements are sentences that tell about something. Statements begin with a capital letter and end with a period. **Questions** are sentences that ask about something. Questions begin with a capital letter and end with a question mark.

Directions: Rewrite the sentences using capital letters and either a period or a question mark.

Example: walruses live in the Arctic

Walruses live in the Arctic.

1. are walruses large sea mammals or fish

_____

2. they spend most of their time in the water and on ice

_____

3. are floating sheets of ice called ice floes

_____

4. are walruses related to seals

_____

5. their skin is thick, wrinkled, and almost hairless

_____

Commands

Commands tell someone to do something. **Example: "Be careful."** It can also be written as "Be careful!" if it tells a strong feeling.

Directions: Put a period at the end of the command sentences. Use an exclamation point if the sentence tells a strong feeling. Write your own commands on the lines below.

1. Clean your room

2. Now

3. Be careful with your goldfish

4. Watch out

5. Be a little more careful

_____

_____

Questions

Questions are sentences that ask something. They begin with a capital letter and end with a question mark.

Directions: Write the questions on the lines below. Begin each sentence with a capital letter and end it with a question mark.

1. will you be my friend

_____

2. what is your name

_____

3. are you eight years old

_____

4. do you like rainbows

_____

Name _____

Main Idea

Directions: Circle the sentence in each paragraph that does not support the main idea.

The school picnic was so much fun! When we arrived, we each made a name tag. Then we signed up for the contests we wanted to enter. My best friend was my partner for every contest. The hen laid so many eggs that I needed a basket to carry them. All that exercise made us very hungry. We were glad to see those tables full of food.

The storm howled outside, so we stayed in for an evening of fun. The colorful rainbow stretched across the sky. The dining room table was stacked with games and puzzles. The delightful smell of popcorn led us into the kitchen where Dad led a parade around the kitchen table. Then we carried our bowls of popcorn into the dining room. We laughed so hard and ate so much, we didn't care who won the games. It was a great evening!

The city championship game would be played on Saturday at Brookside Park. Coach Metzger called an extra practice Friday evening. He said he knew we were good, because we had made it this far. He didn't want us to get nervous and forget everything we knew. School starts on Monday, but I'm not ready to go back yet. After working on some drills, Coach told us to relax, get lots of rest, and come back ready to play.

Main Idea: Chewing Gum

Directions: Read about chewing gum, then answer the questions.

Thomas Adams was an American inventor. In 1870, he was looking for a substitute for rubber. He was working with **chicle** (chick-ul), a substance that comes from a certain kind of tree in Mexico. Years ago, Mexicans chewed chicle. Thomas Adams decided to try it for himself. He liked it so much he started selling it. Twenty years later, he owned a large factory that produced chewing gum.

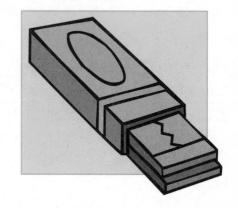

1. Who was the American inventor who started selling chewing gum? _____

2. What was he hoping to invent? _____

3. When did he invent chewing gum? _____

4. Where does the chicle come from? _____

5. Why did Thomas Adams start selling chewing gum? _____

6. How long was it until Adams owned a large factory that produced chewing gum? _____

Name _____

Main Idea: Clay Homes

Directions: Read about adobe houses, then answer the questions.

Pueblo Native Americans live in houses made of clay. They are called **adobe** (ah-doe-bee) **houses.** Adobe is a yellow-colored clay that comes from the ground. The hot sun in New Mexico and Arizona helps dry the clay to make strong bricks. The Pueblos have used adobe to build their homes for many years.

Pueblos use adobe for other purposes, too. The women in the tribes make beautiful pottery out of adobe. While the clay is still damp, they form it into shapes. After they have made the bowls and other containers, they paint them with lovely designs.

1. What is the subject of this story? _____

2. Who uses clay to make their houses? _____

3. How long have they been building adobe houses? _____

4. Why do adobe bricks need to be dried? _____

5. How do the Pueblos make pottery from adobe? _____

Noting Details

Directions: Read the story. Then answer the questions.

The giant panda is much smaller than a brown bear or a polar bear. In fact, a horse weighs about four times as much as a giant panda. So why is it called "giant"? It is giant next to another kind of panda called the red panda.

The red panda also lives in China. The red panda is about the size of a fox. It has a long, fluffy, striped tail and beautiful reddish fur. It looks very much like a raccoon.

Many people think the giant pandas are bears. They look like bears. Even the word panda is Chinese for "white bear." But because of its relationship to the red panda, many scientists now believe that the panda is really more like a raccoon!

1. Why is the giant panda called "giant"?

_____

2. Where does the red panda live?

_____

3. How big is the red panda?

_____

4. What animal does the red panda look like?

_____

5. What does the word panda mean?

_____

Name _____

Recalling Details: Nikki's Pets

Directions: Read about Nikki's pets, then answer the questions.

Nikki has two cats, Tiger and Sniffer, and two dogs, Spot and Wiggles. Tiger is an orange striped cat who likes to sleep under a big tree and pretend she is a real tiger. Sniffer is a gray cat who likes to sniff the flowers in Nikki's garden. Spot is a Dalmatian with many black spots. Wiggles is a big furry brown dog who wiggles all over when he is happy.

1. Which dog is brown and furry? _____

2. What color is Tiger? _____

3. What kind of dog is Spot? _____

4. Which cat likes to sniff flowers? _____

5. Where does Tiger like to sleep? _____

6. Who wiggles all over when he is happy? _____

Reading for Details

Directions: Read the story about bike safety. Answer the questions below the story.

Mike has a red bike. He likes his bike. Mike wears a helmet. Mike wears knee pads and elbow pads. They keep him safe. Mike stops at signs. Mike looks both ways. Mike is safe on his bike.

1. What color is Mike's bike? _____

2. Which sentence in the story tells why Mike wears pads and a helmet? Write it here.

_____

3. What else does Mike do to keep safe?

He _____ at signs and _____ both ways.

Name _____

Following Directions

Directions: Read the story. Answer the questions. Try the recipe.

Cows Give Us Milk

Cows live on a farm. The farmer milks the cow to get milk. Many things are made from milk. We make ice cream, sour cream, cottage cheese, and butter from milk. Butter is fun to make! You can learn to make your own butter. First, you need cream. Put the cream in a jar and shake it. Then you need to pour off the liquid. Next, you put the butter in a bowl. Add a little salt and stir! Finally, spread it on crackers and eat!

1. What animal gives us milk? _____

2. What 4 things are made from milk?
_____ _____ _____ _____

3. What did the story teach you to make? _____

4. Put the steps in order. Place 1, 2, 3, or 4 by the sentence.

_____ Spread the butter on crackers and eat!

_____ Shake cream in a jar.

_____ Start with cream.

_____ Add salt to the butter.

Name _____

Sequencing: 1, 2, 3, 4!

Directions: Write numbers by each sentence to show the order of the story.

The pool is empty. _____   Ben plays in the pool. _____

Ben gets out. _____   Ben fills the pool. _____

Name _____

Sequencing: Yo-Yo Trick

Directions: Read about the yo-yo trick.

Wind up the yo-yo string. Hold the yo-yo in your hand. Now, hold your palm up. Throw the yo-yo downward on the string. Hold your palm down. Now, swing the yo-yo forward. Make it "walk." This yo-yo trick is called "walk the dog."

Directions: Number the directions in order.

_____ Swing the yo-yo forward and make it "walk."

_____ Hold your palm up and drop the yo-yo.

_____ Turn your palm down as the yo-yo reaches the ground.

Sequencing/Predicting: A Game for Cats

Directions: Read about what cats like. Then follow the instructions.

Cats like to play with paper bags. Pull a paper bag open. Take everything out. Now, lay it on its side.

1. Write 1, 2, and 3 to put the pictures in order.

2. In box 4, draw what you think the cat will do.

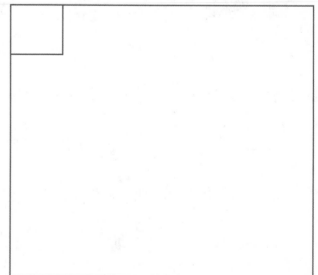

Sequencing: Story Events

Mari was sick yesterday.

Directions: Number the events in 1, 2, 3 order to tell the story about Mari.

_____ She went to the doctor's office.

_____ Mari felt much better.

_____ Mari felt very hot and tired.

_____ Mari's mother went to the drugstore.

_____ The doctor wrote down something.

_____ The doctor looked in Mari's ears.

_____ Mari took a pill.

_____ The doctor gave Mari's mother the piece of paper.

_____ Mari drank some water with her pill.

Sequencing: Why Does It Rain?

Directions: Read about rain, then follow the instructions.

Clouds are made up of little drops of ice and water. They push and bang into each other. Then they join together to make bigger drops and begin to fall. More raindrops cling to them. They become heavy and fall quickly to the ground.

Write **first, second, third, fourth,** and **fifth** to put the events in order.

_____ More raindrops cling to them.

_____ Clouds are made up of little drops of ice and water.

_____ They join together and make bigger drops that begin to fall.

_____ The drops of ice and water bang into each other.

_____ The drops become heavy and fall quickly to the ground.

Sequencing: A Story

This is a story from *The McGuffey Second Reader*. This is a very old book your great-great-grandparents may have used to learn to read.

Directions: Read the story on pages 45 and 46, then answer the questions on page 47.

The Crow and the Robin

One morning in the early spring, a crow was sitting on the branch of an old oak tree. He felt very ugly and cross and could only say, "Croak! Croak!" Soon, a little robin, who was looking for a place to build her nest, came with a merry song into the same tree. "Good morning to you," she said to the crow.

But the crow made no answer; he only looked at the clouds and croaked something about the cold wind. "I said, 'Good morning to you,'" said the robin, jumping from branch to branch.

"I wonder how you can be so merry this morning," croaked the crow.

"Why shouldn't I be merry?" asked the robin. "Spring has come and everyone ought to be happy."

"I am not happy," said the crow. "Don't you see those black clouds above us? It is going to snow."

"Very well," said the robin, "I shall keep on singing until the snow comes. A merry song will not make it any colder."

"Caw, caw, caw," croaked the crow. "I think you are very foolish."

Name _____

Sequencing: A Story

The Crow and the Robin

The robin flew to another tree and kept on singing, but the crow sat still and made himself very unhappy. "The wind is so cold," he said. "It always blows the wrong way for me."

Very soon the sun came out, warm and bright, and the clouds went away, but the crow was as cross as ever.

The grass began to spring up in the meadows. Green leaves and flowers were seen in the woods. Birds and bees flew here and there in the glad sunshine. The crow sat and croaked on the branch of the old oak tree.

"It is always too warm or too cold," said he. "To be sure, it is a little pleasant just now, but I know that the sun will soon shine warm enough to burn me up. Then before night, it will be colder than ever. I do not see how anyone can sing at such a time as this."

Just then the robin came back to the tree with a straw in her mouth for her nest. "Well, my friend," asked she, "where is your snow?"

"Don't talk about that," croaked the crow. "It will snow all the harder for this sunshine."

"And snow or shine," said the robin, "you will keep on croaking. For my part, I shall always look on the bright side of things and have a song for every day in the year."

Which will you be like—the crow or the robin?_____

Sequencing: The Story

These sentences retell the story of "The Crow and the Robin" but are out of order.

Directions: Write the numbers 1 through 10 on he lines to show the correct sequence. The first one has been done for you.

____ Although the sun came out and the clouds went away, the crow was still as cross as ever.

____ "I shall always . . . have a song for every day in the year," said the robin.

_1_ The crow sat on the branch of an old oak tree and could only say, "Croak! Croak!"

____ "This wind is so cold. It always blows the wrong way," the crow said.

____ The crow said, "It is going to snow."

____ The robin said good morning to the crow.

____ The crow told the robin that he thought she was very foolish.

____ The grass began to spring up in the meadows.

____ The robin was jumping from branch to branch as she talked to the crow.

____ The robin came back with straw in her mouth for her nest.

Tracking: Alternate Paths

Look at Spotty Dog's home. Look at the paths he takes to the oven and the back door. The numbers by each path show how many steps Spotty must take to get there.

Directions: Follow the instructions.

1. Spotty Dog's cookies are done. Trace Spotty's path from his chair to the oven.

2. How many steps does Spotty take? _____

3. While Spotty is looking in his oven, he hears a noise in the backyard. Trace Spotty's path to the door.

4. How many steps has Spotty taken in all? _____

5. Spotty goes back to his chair. How many steps must he take? _____

6. How many steps has he taken in all? _____

7. Spotty's path has made a shape. What shape is it? _____

Same/Different: Venn Diagram

A **Venn diagram** is a diagram that shows how two things are the same and different.

Directions: Choose two outdoor sports. Then follow the instructions to complete the Venn diagram.

1. Write the first sport name under the first circle. Write some words that describe the sport. Write them in the first circle.

2. Write the second sport name under the second circle. Write some words that describe the sport. Write them in the circle.

3. Where the 2 circles overlap, write some words that describe both sports.

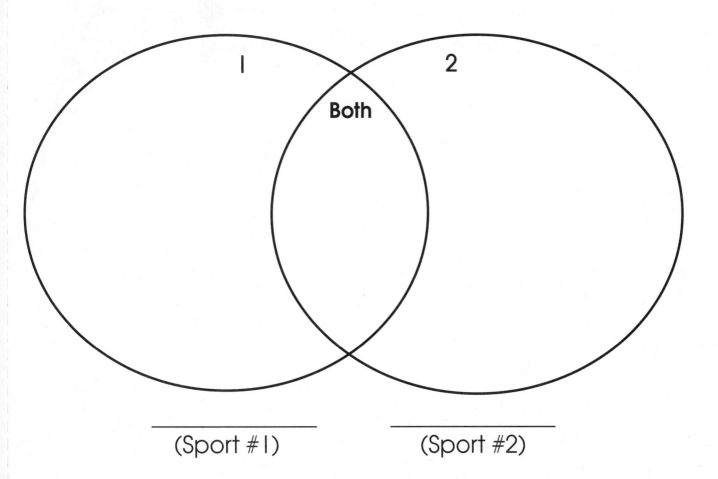

1   2

Both

_____   _____
(Sport #1)   (Sport #2)

Same/Different: Marvin and Mugsy

Directions: Read about Marvin and Mugsy. Then complete the Venn diagram, telling how they are the same and different.

Marcy has two dogs, Marvin and Mugsy. Marvin is a black-and-white spotted Dalmatian. Marvin likes to run after balls in the backyard. His favorite food is Canine Crunchy Crunch. Marcy likes to take Marvin for walks, because dogs need exercise. Marvin loves to sleep in his doghouse. Mugsy is a big furry brown dog, who wiggles when she is happy. Since she is big, she needs lots of exercise. So Marcy takes her for walks in the park. Her favorite food is Canine Crunchy Crunch. Mugsy likes to sleep on Marcy's bed.

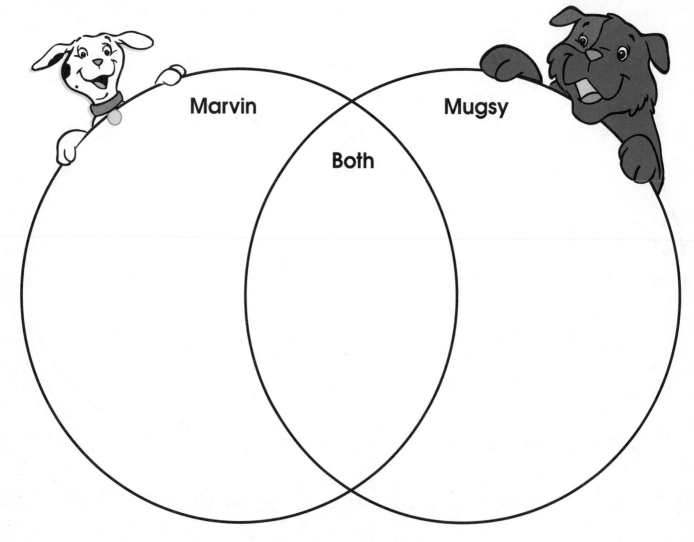

Same/Different: Ann and Lee Have Fun

Directions: Read about Ann and Lee. Then write how they are the same and different in the Venn diagram.

Ann and Lee like to play ball. They like to jump rope. Lee likes to play a card game called "Old Maid." Ann likes to play a card game called "Go Fish." What do you do to have fun?

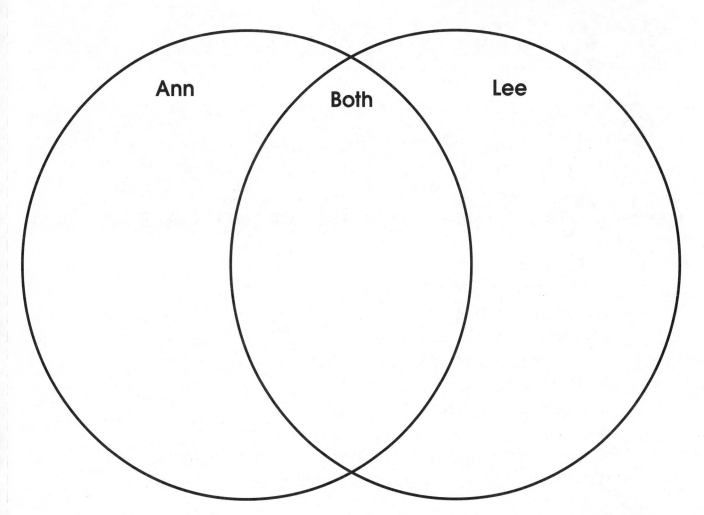

Ann   **Both**   **Lee**

51   Summer Link Reading Grade 3

Classifying

Directions: Read each animal story. Then look at the fun facts. Write an **H** for horse, **P** for panda, or **D** for dog next to each fact.

Horses

Horses are fun to ride. You can ride them in the woods or in fields. Horses usually have pretty names. Sometimes, if they are golden, they are called Amber. Horses swish their tails when it is hot. That keeps the flies away from them.

Pandas

Pandas are from China. They like to climb trees. They scratch bark to write messages to their friends in the trees. When pandas get hungry, they gnaw on bamboo shoots.

Dogs

Dogs are good pets. People often call them by names like Spot or Fido. Sometimes they are named after their looks. For example, a brown dog is sometimes named Brownie. Some people have special, small doors for their dogs to use.

Fun Facts

_____ 1. My name is often Spot or Fido.

_____ 2. I am from China.

_____ 3. I make a good house pet.

_____ 4. I like to carry people into the fields.

_____ 5. My favorite food is bamboo.

_____ 6. Flies bother me when I am hot.

_____ 7. Amber is often my name when I am golden.

_____ 8. I leave messages for my friends by scratching bark.

_____ 9. Sometimes I have my own special door on a house.

Classifying

Classifying is putting similar things into groups.

Directions: Write each word from the word box on the correct line.

baby	donkey	whale	family	fox
uncle	goose	grandfather	kangaroo	policeman

people   animal

_____   _____

_____   _____

_____   _____

_____   _____

_____   _____

Classifying: Watch Out for Poison Ivy!

Poison ivy is not safe. If you touch it, it can make your skin red and itchy. It can hurt. It grows on the ground. It has three leaves. It can be green or red. Watch out, Jay! There is poison ivy in these woods.

Directions: Color the poison ivy leaves red. Then color the "safe" leaves other colors.

Name _____

Comprehension: Sea Horses Look Strange!

Directions: Read about sea horses. Then answer the questions.

Sea horses are fish, not horses. A sea horse's head looks like a horse's head. It has a tail like a monkey's tail. A sea horse looks very strange!

1. (Circle the correct answer.)
   A sea horse is a kind of

        horse.

        monkey.

        fish.

2. What does a sea horse's head look like?

_____

_____

3. What makes a sea horse look strange?

a. _____

b. _____

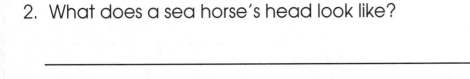

Name _____

Comprehension: How to Stop a Dog Fight

Directions: Read about how to stop a dog fight. Then answer the questions.

Sometimes dogs fight. They bark loudly. They may bite. Do not try to pull apart fighting dogs. Turn on a hose and spray them with water. This will stop the fight.

1. Name some things dogs may do if they are mad.

_____

_____

2. Why is it unwise to pull on dogs that are fighting?

_____

_____

3. Do you think dogs like to get wet?

_____

Comprehension: A Winter Story

Directions: Read about winter. Then follow the instructions.

It is cold in winter. Snow falls. Water freezes. Most kids like to play outdoors. Some kids make a snowman. Some kids skate. What do you do in winter?

1. Circle the main idea:

   Snow falls in winter.

   In winter, there are many things to do outside.

2. Write two things about winter weather.

   1) _____

   2) _____

3. Write what you like to do in winter.

   _____

   _____

   _____

   _____

   _____

   _____

Comprehension: More About Snakes!

Directions: Read more about snakes. Then follow the instructions.

Unlike people, snakes have cold blood. They like to be warm. They hunt for food when it is warm. They lie in the sun. When it is cold, snakes curl up into a ball.

1. What do snakes do when it is warm?

    a. _____

    b. _____

2. Why do you think snakes curl up when it is cold? _____

    _____

3. (Circle the correct answer.)

People have: (cold blood / warm blood).

Comprehension: Ant Farms

Directions: Read about ant farms. Then answer the questions.

Ant farms are sold at toy stores and pet stores. Ant farms come in a flat frame. The frame has glass on each side. Inside the glass is sand. The ants live in the sand.

1. Where are ant farms sold? _____

2. The frame has _____ on each side.

Circle the correct answer.

3. The ants live in (water / sand).

4. The ant farm frame is (flat / round).

Comprehension: Sharks Are Fish, Too!

Directions: Read the story. Then follow the instructions.

Angela learned a lot about sharks when her class visited the city aquarium. She learned that sharks are fish. Some sharks are as big as an elephant, and some can fit into a small paper bag. Sharks have no bones. They have hundreds of teeth, and when they lose them, they grow new ones. They eat animals of any kind. Whale sharks are the largest of all fish.

1. Circle the main idea:

   Angela learned a lot about sharks at the aquarium.

   Some sharks are as big as elephants.

2. When sharks lose teeth, they _____

   _____

3. _____ are the largest of all fish.

4. Sharks have bones. (Circle the answer.)

   Yes   No

Name _____

Comprehension: Outdoor/Indoor Games

Directions: Read the story. Then answer the questions.

Derrick likes to play outdoor and indoor games. His favorite outdoor game is baseball because he likes to hit the ball with the bat and run around the bases. He plays this game in the park with the neighborhood kids.

When it rains, he plays checkers with Lorenzo on the dining-room table in his apartment. He likes the game, because he has to use his brain to think about his next move, and the rules are easy to follow.

1. What is your favorite outdoor game? _____

2. Why do you like this game? _____

_____

3. Where is this game played? _____

4. What is your favorite indoor game? _____

5. Why do you like this game? _____

_____

6. Where is this game played? _____

61   Summer Link Reading Grade 3

Comprehension: Early Trucks

What would we do without trucks? Your family may not own a truck, but everyone depends on trucks. Trucks bring our food to stores. Trucks deliver our furniture. Trucks carry new clothes to shopping centers. The goods of the world move on trucks.

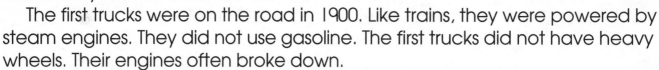

Trucks are harder to make than cars. They must be sturdy. They carry heavy loads. They cannot break down.

The first trucks were on the road in 1900. Like trains, they were powered by steam engines. They did not use gasoline. The first trucks did not have heavy wheels. Their engines often broke down.

Trucks changed when the U.S. entered World War I in 1917. Big, heavy tires were put on trucks. Gasoline engines were used. Trucks used in war had to be sturdy. Lives were at stake!

Directions: Answer these questions about the first trucks.

1. What powered the first trucks?

_____

2. When did early trucks begin using gasoline engines?

_____

3. How do trucks serve us?

_____

_____

4. Why did trucks used in war have to be sturdy?

_____

Predicting: A Rainy Game

Predicting is telling what is likely to happen based on the facts.

Directions: Read the story. Then check each sentence below that tells how the story could end.

   One cloudy day, Juan and his baseball team, the Bears, played the Crocodiles. It was the last half of the fifth inning, and it started to rain. The coaches and umpires had to decide what to do.

_____ They kept playing until nine innings were finished.

_____ They ran for cover and waited until the rain stopped.

_____ Each player grabbed an umbrella and returned to the field to finish the game.

_____ They canceled the game and played it another day.

_____ They acted like crocodiles and slid around the wet bases.

_____ The coaches played the game while the players sat in the dugout.

Predicting Outcome

Directions: Read the story. Complete the story in the last box.

1. "Look at that elephant! He sure is big!"

2. "I'm hungry." "I bet that elephant is, too."

3. "Stop, Amy! Look at that sign!"

4. _____
   _____
   _____

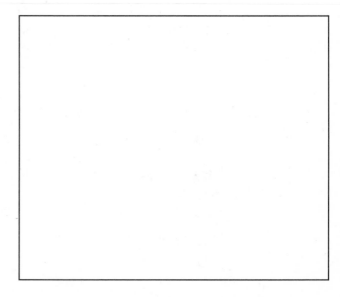

Fact and Opinion

A **fact** is something that can be proven. An **opinion** is a feeling or belief about something and cannot be proven.

Directions: Read these sentences about different games. Then write **F** next to each fact and **O** next to each opinion.

_____ 1. Tennis is cool!

_____ 2. There are red and black markers in a Checkers game.

_____ 3. In football, a touchdown is worth six points.

_____ 4. Being a goalie in soccer is easy.

_____ 5. A yo-yo moves on a string.

_____ 6. June's sister looks like the queen on the card.

_____ 7. The six kids need three more players for a baseball team.

_____ 8. Table tennis is more fun than court tennis.

_____ 9. Hide-and-Seek is a game that can be played outdoors or indoors.

_____ 10. Play money is used in many board games.

Name _____

Fact and Opinion

Directions: Read the story. Then follow the instructions.

Tashi's family likes to go to the zoo. Her favorite animals are all the different kinds of birds. Tashi likes birds because they can fly, they have colorful feathers, and they make funny noises.

Write **F** next to each fact and **O** next to each opinion.

_____ 1. Birds have two feet.

_____ 2. All birds lay eggs.

_____ 3. Parrots are too noisy.

_____ 4. All birds have feathers and wings.

_____ 5. It would be great to be a bird and fly south for the winter.

_____ 6. Birds have hard beaks or bills instead of teeth.

_____ 7. Pigeons are fun to watch.

_____ 8. Some birds cannot fly.

_____ 9. Parakeets make good pets.

_____ 10. A penguin is a bird.

Making Inferences

Directions: Read the story. Then answer the questions.

Mrs. Sweet looked forward to a visit from her niece, Candy. In the morning, she cleaned her house. She also baked a cherry pie. An hour before Candy was to arrive, the phone rang. Mrs. Sweet said, "I understand." When she hung up the phone, she looked very sad.

1. Who do you think called Mrs. Sweet?

_____

_____

2. How do you know that?

_____

_____

3. Why is Mrs. Sweet sad?

_____

_____

Making Inferences

Juniper has three problems to solve. She needs your help.

Directions: Read each problem. Write what you think she should do.

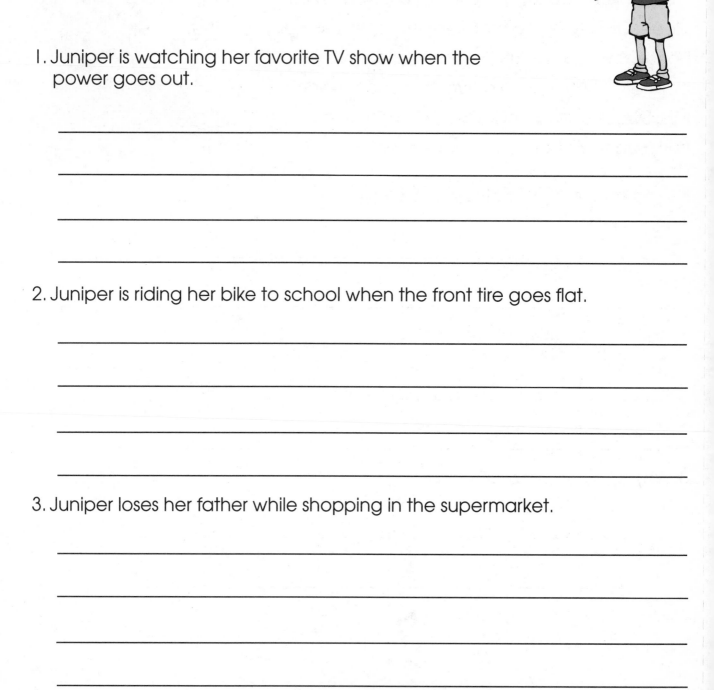

1. Juniper is watching her favorite TV show when the power goes out.

_____

_____

_____

_____

2. Juniper is riding her bike to school when the front tire goes flat.

_____

_____

_____

_____

3. Juniper loses her father while shopping in the supermarket.

_____

_____

_____

_____

Making Inferences

Help make a "doggie pizza" for Spotty Dog. The steps to follow are all mixed-up. Three of the steps are not needed.

Directions: Number the steps in order from 1 to 7. Draw a dog bone by the 3 steps that are not needed.

_____ Place the dough on a round pan.

_____ Cover the top with cheese.

_____ Take a nap.

_____ Make the pizza dough.

_____ Run out the door.

_____ Bake it in a hot oven.

_____ Roll the dough out flat.

_____ Play ball with Spotty.

_____ Spread the sauce on the dough.

_____ Sprinkle bits of dog biscuits on top.

Directions: Draw Spotty Dog's pizza in the box.

Making Deductions

Dad is cooking dinner tonight. You can find out what day of the week it is.

Directions: Read the clues. Complete the menu. Answer the question.

Menu
Monday _____
Tuesday _____
Wednesday _____
Thursday _____
Friday _____
Saturday _____
Sunday _____

1. Mom fixed pizza on Monday.
2. Dad fixed cheese rolls the day before that.
3. Tess made meat pie three days after Mom fixed pizza.
4. Tom fixed corn-on-the-cob the day before Tess made meat pie.
5. Mom fixed hot dogs the day after Tess made meat pie.
6. Tess cooked fish the day before Dad fixed cheese rolls.
7. Dad is making chicken today. What day is it? _____

Drawing Conclusions: Mrs. Posy's Roses

Directions: Read more about Mrs. Posy, then answer the questions.

Mrs. Posy is working in her rose garden. She is trimming the branches so that the plants will grow better. Mrs. Posy is careful, because rose bushes have thorns on them. "Hello, Mrs. Posy!" calls Ann as she rides her bicycle down the street. "Hi, Ann!" replies Mrs. Posy. Then she yells, "Ouch!" She runs inside the house and stays there for a few minutes. When Mrs. Posy comes back outside, she has a bandage on one finger.

1. Why is Mrs. Posy careful when she works with rose bushes?

_____

2. Why does Mrs. Posy look up from her work? _____

_____

3. Why did Mrs. Posy yell, "Ouch!"? _____

_____

4. Why did Mrs. Posy run into the house? _____

_____

Drawing Conclusions: Eskimos

Directions: Read about the traditional lives of Eskimos, then answer the questions.

Eskimos live in Alaska. A long time ago, Eskimos lived in houses made of snow, dirt, or animal skins. They moved around from place to place. The Eskimos hunted and fished. They often ate raw meat because they had no way to cook it. When they ate meat raw, they liked it dried or frozen. Eskimos used animal skins for their clothes. They used fat from whales, seals, and other animals to heat their houses.

1. Why did the Eskimos make houses out of snow? _____

_____

2. How did they prepare their raw meat? _____

_____

3. How might they use animal fat to heat their houses? _____

_____

Review

Directions: Read the story. Then answer the questions.

Randa, Emily, Ali, Dave, Liesl, and Deana all love to read. Every Tuesday, they all go to the library together and pick out their favorite books. Randa likes books about fish. Emily likes books about sports and athletes. Ali likes books about art. Dave likes books about wild animals. Liesl likes books with riddles and puzzles. Deanna likes books about cats and dogs.

1. Circle the main idea:

   Randa, Emily, Ali, Dave, Liesl, and Deana are good friends.

   Randa, Emily, Ali, Dave, Liesl, and Deana all like books.

2. Who do you think might grow up to be an artist?

   _____

3. Who do you think might grow up to be an oceanographer (someone who studies the ocean)?

   _____

4. Who do you think might grow up to be a veterinarian (an animal doctor)?

   _____

5. Who do you think might grow up to be a zookeeper (someone who cares for zoo animals)?

   _____

Name _____

Cause and Effect

1. Our telephone was not working, so I called the doctor from next door.

2. The police officer began to direct traffic, since the traffic signal was not working.

3. The class will go out to recess when the room is cleaned up.

4. "I can't see you because the room is too dark," said Jordan.

5. He has to wash the dishes alone because his sister is sick.

6. Since the bus had engine trouble, several children were late to school.

7. Monday was a holiday, so Mom and Dad took us to the park.

Compare and Contrast

To **compare** means to discuss how things are similar. To **contrast** means to discuss how things are different.

Directions: Compare and contrast how people grow gardens. Write at least two answers for each question.

Many people in the country have large gardens. They have a lot of space, so they can plant many kinds of vegetables and flowers. Since the gardens are usually quite large, they use a wheelbarrow to carry the tools they need. Sometimes they even have to carry water or use a garden hose.

People who live in the city do not always have enough room for a garden. Many people in big cities live in apartment buildings. They can put in a window

box or use part of their balcony space to grow things. Most of the time, the only garden tools they need are a hand trowel to loosen the dirt and a watering can to make sure the plant gets enough water.

1. Compare gardening in the country with gardening in the city.

   _____

   _____

2. Contrast gardening in the country with gardening in the city.

   _____

   _____

Fiction and Nonfiction

Fiction writing is a story that has been invented. The story might be about things that could really happen (realistic) or about things that couldn't possibly happen (fantasy). **Nonfiction** writing is based on facts. It usually gives information about people, places, or things. A person can often tell while reading whether a story or book is fiction or nonfiction.

Directions: Read the paragraphs below and on page 77. Determine whether each paragraph is fiction or nonfiction. Circle the letter **F** for fiction or the letter **N** for nonfiction.

"Do not be afraid, little flowers," said the oak. "Close your yellow eyes in sleep and trust in me. You have made me glad many a time with your sweetness. Now, I will take care that the winter shall do you no harm." **F N**

The whole team watched as the ball soared over the outfield fence. The game was over! It was hard to walk off the field and face parents, friends, and each other. It had been a long season. Now, they would have to settle for second place. **F N**

Be careful when you remove the dish from the microwave. It will be very hot, so take care not to get burned by the dish or the hot steam. If time permits, leave the dish in the microwave for 2 or 3 minutes to avoid getting burned. It is a good idea to use a potholder, too. **F N**

Fiction and Nonfiction

Megan and Mariah skipped out to the playground. They enjoyed playing together at recess. Today, it was Mariah's turn to choose what they would do first. To Megan's surprise, Mariah asked, "What do you want to do, Megan? I'm going to let you pick since it's your birthday!" **F N**

It is easy to tell an insect from a spider. An insect has three body parts and six legs. A spider has eight legs and no wings. Of course, if you see the creature spinning a web, you will know what it is. An insect wouldn't want to get too close to the web or it would be stuck. It might become dinner! **F N**

My name is Lee Chang, and I live in a country that you call China. My home is on the other side of the world from yours. When the sun is rising in my country, it is setting in yours. When it is day at your home, it is night at mine. **F N**

Henry washed the dog's foot in cold water from the brook. The dog lay very still, for he knew that the boy was trying to help him. **F N**

77   **Summer Link Reading Grade 3**

Fantasy and Reality

Something that is **real** could actually happen. Something that is **fantasy** is not real. It could not happen.

Examples: **Real:** Dogs can bark.
                Fantasy: Dogs can fly.

Directions: Look at the sentences below. Write **real** or **fantasy** next to each sentence.

1. My cat can talk to me.   _____

2. Witches ride brooms and cast spells.   _____

3. Dad can mow the lawn.   _____

4. I ride a magic carpet to school.   _____

5. I have a man-eating tree.   _____

6. My sandbox has toys in it.   _____

7. Mom can bake chocolate chip cookies.   _____

8. Mark's garden has tomatoes and corn in it.   _____

9. Jack grows candy and ice cream
   in his garden.   _____

10. I make my bed everyday.   _____

Write your own **real** sentence.   _____

_____

Write your own **fantasy** sentence.   _____

_____

Learning Dictionary Skills

A dictionary is a book that gives the meaning of words. It also tells how words sound. Words in a dictionary are in alphabetical order. That makes them easier to find. A picture dictionary lists a word, a picture of the word, and its meaning.

Directions: Look at this page from a picture dictionary, then answer the questions.

baby

A very young child.

band

A group of people who play music.

bank

A place where money is kept.

bark

The sound a dog makes.

berry

A small, juicy fruit.

board

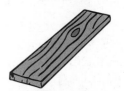

A flat piece of wood.

1. What is a small, juicy fruit? _____

2. What is a group of people who play music? _____

3. What is the name for a very young child? _____

4. What is a flat piece of wood called? _____

Making Inferences: Dictionary Mystery

Directions: Below are six dictionary entries with pronunciations and definitions. The only things missing are the entry words. Write the correct entry words. Be sure to spell each word correctly.

Entry word:

_____

(rōz)
A flower that grows on bushes and vines.

Entry word:

_____

(fäks)
A wild animal that lives in the woods.

Entry word:

_____

(lāk)
A body of water that is surrounded by land.

Entry word:

_____

(ra bət)
A small animal that has long ears.

Entry word:

_____

(pē än ō)
A musical instrument that has many keys.

Entry word:

_____

(bās bȯl)
A game played with a bat and a ball.

Directions: Now write the entry words in alphabetical order.

1. _____

2. _____

3. _____

4. _____

5. _____

6. _____

Reading for Information: Newspapers

A newspaper has many parts. Some of the parts of a newspaper are:

- banner — the name of the paper
- lead story — the top news item
- caption — sentences under the picture which give information about the picture
- sports — scores and information on current sports events
- comics — drawings that tell funny stories
- editorial — an article by the editor expressing an opinion about something
- ads — paid advertisements
- weather — information about the weather
- advice column — letters from readers asking for help with a problem
- movie guides — a list of movies and movie times
- obituary — information about people who have died

Directions: Match the newspaper sections below with their definitions.

banner	an article by the editor
lead story	sentences under pictures
caption	movies and movie times
editorial	the name of the paper
movies	information about people who have died
obituary	the top news item

Library Skills: Alphabetical Order

Ms. Ling, the school librarian, needs help shelving books. Fiction titles are arranged in alphabetical order by the author's last name. Ms. Ling has done the first set for you.

__3__ Silverstein, Shel   __1__ Bridwell, Norman   __2__ Farley, Walter

Directions: Number the following groups of authors in alphabetical order.

_____ Bemelmans, Ludwig   _____ Perkins, Al

_____ Stein, R.L.   _____ Dobbs, Rose

_____ Sawyer, Ruth   _____ Baldwin, James

_____ Baum, L. Frank   _____ Kipling, Rudyard

The content of some books is also arranged alphabetically.

Directions: Circle the books that are arranged in alphabetical order.

T.V. guide   dictionary   encyclopedia   novel

almanac   science book   Yellow Pages   catalog

Write the books you circled in alphabetical order.

1._____

2._____

3._____

Periodicals

Libraries also have periodicals such as magazines and newspapers. They are called **periodicals** because they are printed regularly within a set period of time. There are many kinds of magazines. Some discuss the news. Others cover fitness, cats, or other topics of special interest. Almost every city or town has a newspaper. Newspapers usually are printed daily, weekly, or even monthly. Newspapers cover what is happening in your town and in the world. They usually include sections on sports and entertainment. They present a lot of information.

Directions: Follow the instructions.

1. Choose an interesting magazine.

   What is the name of the magazine? _____

   List the titles of three articles in the magazine.

   _____

   _____

   _____

2. Now, look at a newspaper.

   What is the name of the newspaper? _____

   The title of a newspaper story is called a headline.

   What are some of the headlines in your local

   newspaper?

   _____

   _____

   _____

Reading a Schedule

Special Saturday classes are being offered to students of the county schools. They will be given the chance to choose from art, music or gymnastics classes.

Directions: Read the schedule, then answer the questions.

	Saturday, November 13	
Art	**Music**	**Gymnastics**
8:00 A.M. Watercolor—Room 350 Clay Sculpting—Room 250	Island Rhythms—Room 54 Orchestra Instruments—Stage	Floor Exercises—W. Gym Parallel Bars—E. Gym
Break (10 minutes)		
10:00 A.M. Painting Stills—Room 420 Watercolor—Room 350	Percussion—Room 54 Jazz Sounds—Stage	Uneven Bars—N. Gym _____
Break (10 minutes)		
11:00 A.M. Oils on Canvas—Room 258 _____	Island Rhythms—Room 54 Create Your Own Music— Room 40	Uneven Bars—N. Gym Balance Beam—W. Gym

1. Where would you meet to learn about Jazz Sounds? _____

2. Could a student sign up for Watercolor and Floor Exercises? _____
   Explain your answer. _____

3. Which music class would a creative person enjoy? _____

   _____

4. Could a person sign up for an art class at 11:00? _____

5. What time is the class on clay sculpting offered? _____

Glossary of Reading and Language Arts Terms

adjective: a describing word that tells more about a noun

adverb: tells when, where, or how about the verb of a sentence

antonym: words with opposite, or nearly opposite, meanings

articles: any one of the words *a, an,* or *the* used to modify a noun

base word (also called root word): the word left after you take off a prefix or a suffix

character: a person, animal, or object that a story is about

climax: the most thrilling part of the story where the problem will or will not be solved

conclusion: a final decision about something, or the part of a story that tells what happens to the characters

contraction: shortened forms of two words often using an apostrophe to show where letters are missing

consonant blend: two or three consonant letters whose sounds combine in a word

diphthongs: two vowels together that make a new sound

fact: something known to be true

fiction: stories that are made up

homophone: a word with the same pronunciation as another, but with a different meaning, and often a different spelling, such as *sun–son*

nonfiction: stories that are true

noun: a word that names a person, place, or thing

opinion: a belief based on what a person thinks instead of what is known to be true

plot: explains the events in a story that create a problem

plural: a form of a word that names or refers to more than one person or thing

predicate: the part of the sentence that tells what the subject does

prefix: a part that is added to the beginning of a word that changes the word's meaning

pronoun: a word that is used in place of a noun

punctuation: the marks that qualify sentences, such as a period, comma, question mark, exclamation, and apostrophe

setting: the place and time that a story happens

subject: the person, place, or thing that the sentence is about

suffix: a part added to the end of a word to change the word's meaning

synonym: word that mean the same, or almost the same, thing

verb: a word that can show action

verb tense: tells whether the action is happening in the past, present, or future

Page 5

Consonant Teams

Consonant teams are two or three consonant letters that have a single sound. **Examples: sh** and **tch**

Directions: Write each word from the word box next to its picture. Underline the consonant team in each word. Circle the consonant team in each word in the box.

bench	match	shoe	thimble
shell	brush	peach	watch
whale	teeth	chair	wheel

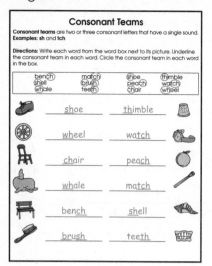

shoe — thimble
wheel — watch
chair — peach
whale — match
bench — shell
brush — teeth

Page 6

Consonant Teams

Directions: Circle the consonant teams in each word in the word box. Write a word from the word box to finish each sentence. Circle the consonant teams in your words.

trash	splash	chain
shut	chicken	catch
ship	when	patch
	which	

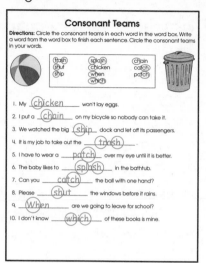

1. My chicken won't lay eggs.
2. I put a chain on my bicycle so nobody can take it.
3. We watched the big ship dock and let off its passengers.
4. It is my job to take out the trash.
5. I have to wear a patch over my eye until it is better.
6. The baby likes to splash in the bathtub.
7. Can you catch the ball with one hand?
8. Please shut the windows before it rains.
9. When are we going to leave for school?
10. I don't know which of these books is mine.

Page 7

Double Vowel Words

Usually when two vowels appear together, the first one says its name and the second one is silent.

Example: bean

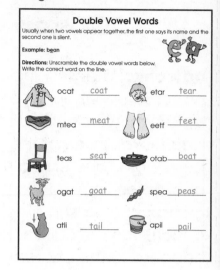

Directions: Unscramble the double vowel words below. Write the correct word on the line.

ocat — coat   etar — tear
mtea — meat   eetf — feet
teas — seat   otab — boat
ogat — goat   spea — peas
atli — tail   apil — pail

Page 8

Silent Letters

Some words have letters you can not hear at all, such as the **gh** in **night**, the **w** in **wrong**, the **l** in **walk**, the **k** in **knee**, the **b** in **climb**, and the **t** in **listen**.

Directions: Look at the words in the word box. Write the word under its picture. Underline the silent letters.

knife	light	calf	wrench	lamb	eight
wrist	whistle	comb	thumb	knob	knee

eight — wrist — knee — calf
lamb — knob — whistle — light
wrench — comb — thumb — knife

Page 9

Review

Directions: Read the story. Circle the consonant teams (two or three letters) and silent letters in the underlined words. Be sure to check for more than one team in a word! One has been done for you.

One day last spring, my family went on a picnic. My father picked out a pretty spot next to a stream. While my brother and I climbed a tree, my mother spread out a sheet and placed the food on it. But before we could eat, a skunk walked out of the woods! Mother screamed and scared the skunk. It sprayed us with a terrible smell! Now, we think it is a funny story. But that day, we ran!

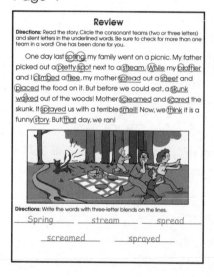

Directions: Write the words with three-letter blends on the lines.

Spring — stream — spread
screamed — sprayed

Page 10

Review

Directions: Look through a magazine. Cut out pictures of nouns and glue them below. Write the name of the noun next to the picture.

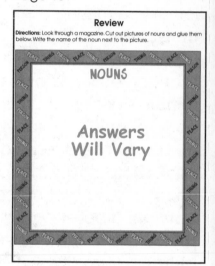

NOUNS

Answers Will Vary

Page 11

Plurals

Plurals are words that mean more than one. You usually add an **s** or **es** to the word. In some words ending in **y**, the **y** changes to an **i** before adding **es**. For example, **baby** changes to **babies**.

Directions: Look at the following lists of plural words. Write the word that means one next to it. The first one has been done for you.

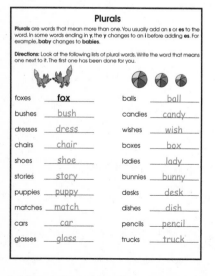

foxes	**fox**	balls	ball
bushes	bush	candles	candy
dresses	dress	wishes	wish
chairs	chair	boxes	box
shoes	shoe	ladies	lady
stories	story	bunnies	bunny
puppies	puppy	desks	desk
matches	match	dishes	dish
cars	car	pencils	pencil
glasses	glass	trucks	truck

Page 12

Compound Subjects

Two similar sentences can be joined into one sentence if the predicate is the same. A **compound subject** is made up of two subjects joined together by the word **and**.

Example: Jamie can sing.
Sandy can sing.
Jamie **and** Sandy can sing.

Directions: Combine the sentences. Write the new sentence on the line.

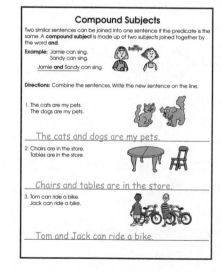

1. The cats are my pets.
The dogs are my pets.

The cats and dogs are my pets.

2. Chairs are in the store.
Tables are in the store.

Chairs and tables are in the store.

3. Tom can ride a bike.
Jack can ride a bike.

Tom and Jack can ride a bike.

Page 13

Verbs

Directions: Write each verb in the correct column.

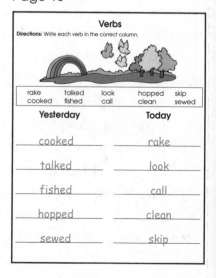

rake	talked	look	hopped	skip
cooked	fished	call	clean	sewed

Yesterday	Today
cooked	rake
talked	look
fished	call
hopped	clean
sewed	skip

Page 14

Compound Subjects and Predicates

The following sentences have either a **compound subject** or a **compound predicate**.

Directions: If the sentence has a compound subject (more than one thing doing the action), **underline** the subject. If it has a compound predicate (more than one action), **circle** the predicate.

Example: <u>Bats and owls</u> like the night.

The fox (slinks and spies)

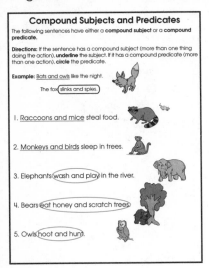

1. <u>Raccoons and mice</u> steal food.

2. <u>Monkeys and birds</u> sleep in trees.

3. Elephants (wash and play) in the river.

4. Bears (eat honey and scratch trees)

5. Owls (hoot and hunt)

Page 15

Ownership

Directions: Read the sentences. Choose the correct word and write it in the sentences below.

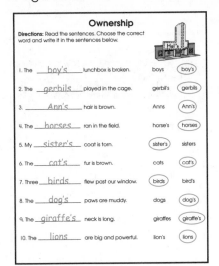

1. The __boy's__ lunchbox is broken.   boys   (boy's)

2. The __gerbils__ played in the cage.   gerbil's   (gerbils)

3. __Ann's__ hair is brown.   Anns   (Ann's)

4. The __horses__ ran in the field.   horse's   (horses)

5. My __sister's__ coat is torn.   (sister's)   sisters

6. The __cat's__ fur is brown.   cats   (cat's)

7. Three __birds__ flew past our window.   (birds)   bird's

8. The __dog's__ paws are muddy.   dogs   (dog's)

9. The __giraffe's__ neck is long.   giraffes   (giraffe's)

10. The __lions__ are big and powerful.   lion's   (lions)

Page 16

Synonyms

Directions: Read each sentence. Fill in the blanks with the synonyms.

friend	tired	story
presents	little	

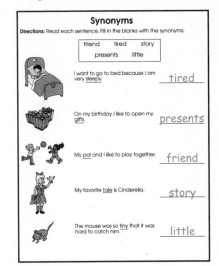

I want to go to bed because I am very <u>sleepy</u>.   __tired__

On my birthday I like to open my <u>gifts</u>.   __presents__

My <u>pal</u> and I like to play together.   __friend__

My favorite <u>tale</u> is Cinderella.   __story__

The mouse was so <u>tiny</u> that it was hard to catch him.   __little__

Page 17

Antonyms

Antonyms are words that are opposites.

Directions: Read the words next to the pictures. Draw a line to the antonyms.

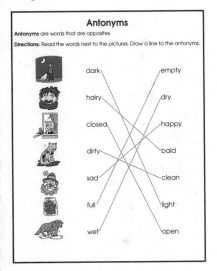

dark — light
hairy — bald
closed — open
dirty — clean
sad — happy
full — empty
wet — dry

Page 18

Antonyms: Completing a Story

Directions: Write opposite words in the blanks to complete the story.

hot	hard	top	cold	bottom
soft	quickly	happy	slowly	sad

One day, Grandma came for a visit. She gave my sister Jenny and me a box of chocolate candy. We said, "Thank you!" Then Jenny __quickly__ took the __top__ off the box. The pieces all looked the same! I couldn't tell which pieces were __soft__ inside and which were __hard__! I only liked the __soft__ ones. Jenny didn't care. She was __happy__ to get any kind of candy! I __slowly__ looked at all the pieces. I didn't know which one to pick. Just then Dad called us. Grandma was going home. He wanted us to say good-bye to her. I hurried to the front door where they were standing. Jenny came a minute later.

I told Grandma I hoped I would see her soon. I always feel __sad__ when she leaves. Jenny stood behind me and didn't say anything. After Grandma went home, I found out why. Jenny had most of our candy in her mouth! Only a few pieces were left in the __bottom__ of the box! Then I was __sad__! That Jenny!

Page 19

Homophones

Directions: Read each word. Circle the picture that goes with the word.

1. sun
2. ate
3. buy
4. hi
5. four
6. hear

Page 20

Is, Are, and Am

is, **are**, and **am** are special action words that tell us something is happening now.

Use **am** with I. **Example:** I am.
Use **is** to tell about one person or thing. **Example:** He is.
Use **are** to tell about more than one. **Example:** We are.
Use **are** with **you**. **Example:** You are.

Directions: Write **is**, **are**, or **am** in the sentences below.

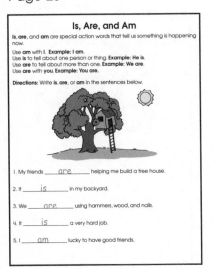

1. My friends __are__ helping me build a tree house.

2. It __is__ in my backyard.

3. We __are__ using hammers, wood, and nails.

4. It __is__ a very hard job.

5. I __am__ lucky to have good friends.

Page 21

Was and Were

Was and **were** tell us about something that already happened.

Use **was** to tell about one person or thing. **Example:** I was, he was. Use **were** to tell about more than one person or thing or when using the word you. **Example:** We were, you were.

Directions: Write **was** or **were** in each sentence.

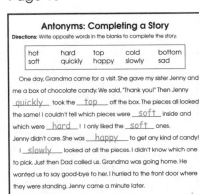

1. Lily __was__ eight years old on her birthday.

2. Tim and Steve __were__ happy to be at the party.

3. Megan __was__ too shy to sing "Happy Birthday."

4. Ben __was__ sorry he dropped his cake.

5. All of the children __were__ happy to be invited.

Page 22

Go, Going, and Went

We use **go** or **going** to tell about now or later. Sometimes we use **going** with the words **am** or **are**. We use **went** to tell about something that already happened.

Directions: Write **go**, **going**, or **went** in the sentences below.

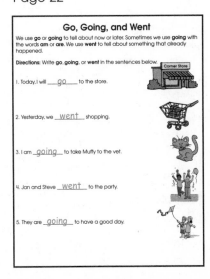

1. Today, I will __go__ to the store.

2. Yesterday, we __went__ shopping.

3. I am __going__ to take Muffy to the vet.

4. Jan and Steve __went__ to the party.

5. They are __going__ to have a good day.

Summer Link Reading Grade 3

Page 23

Have, Has, and Had

We use **have** and **has** to tell about now. We use **had** to tell about something that already happened.

Directions: Write **has**, **have**, or **had** in the sentences below.

1. We ___have___ three cats at home.

2. Ginger ___has___ brown fur.

3. Bucky and Charlie ___have___ gray fur.

4. My friend Tom ___had___ one cat, but he died.

5. Tom ___has___ a new cat now.

Page 24

See, Saw, and Sees

We use **see** or **sees** to tell about now. We use **saw** to tell about something that already happened.

Directions: Write **see**, **sees**, or **saw** in the sentences below.

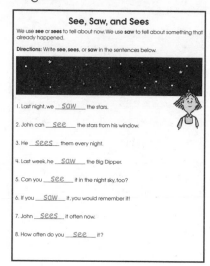

1. Last night, we ___saw___ the stars.

2. John can ___see___ the stars from his window.

3. He ___sees___ them every night.

4. Last week, he ___saw___ the Big Dipper.

5. Can you ___see___ it in the night sky, too?

6. If you ___saw___ it, you would remember it!

7. John ___sees___ it often now.

8. How often do you ___see___ it?

Page 25

Eat, Eats, and Ate

We use **eat** or **eats** to tell about now. We use **ate** to tell about what already happened.

Directions: Write **eat**, **eats**, or **ate** in the sentences below.

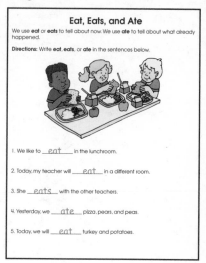

1. We like to ___eat___ in the lunchroom.

2. Today, my teacher will ___eat___ in a different room.

3. She ___eats___ with the other teachers.

4. Yesterday, we ___ate___ pizza, pears, and peas.

5. Today, we will ___eat___ turkey and potatoes.

Page 26

Leave, Leaves, and Left

We use **leave** and **leaves** to tell about now. We use **left** to tell about what already happened.

Directions: Write **leave**, **leaves**, or **left** in the sentences below.

1. Last winter, we ___left___ seeds in the bird feeder everyday.

2. My mother likes to ___leave___ food out for the squirrels.

3. When it rains, she ___leaves___ bread for the birds.

4. Yesterday, she ___left___ popcorn for the birds.

Page 27

Sentences

Directions: Write capital letters where they should appear in the sentences below.

Example: joe can play in january.

1. we celebrate thanksgiving on the third thursday in november.

   We celebrate Thanksgiving on the third Thursday in November.

2. in june, michelle and mark will go camping every friday.

   In June, Michelle and Mark will go camping every Friday.

3. on mondays in october, i will take piano lessons.

   On Mondays in October, I will take piano lessons.

Page 28

Parts of a Sentence

Directions: Look at the pictures. Draw a line from the naming part of the sentence to the action part to complete the sentence.

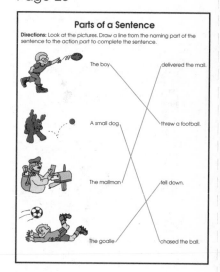

The boy — delivered the mail.

A small dog — threw a football.

The mailman — fell down.

The goalie — chased the ball.

Page 29

Complete the Sentences

Directions: Write your own endings to make the sentences tell a complete idea.

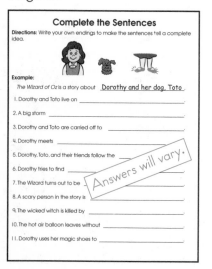

Example:

The Wizard of Oz is a story about ___Dorothy and her dog, Toto___.

1. Dorothy and Toto live on _____

2. A big storm _____

3. Dorothy and Toto are carried off to _____

4. Dorothy meets _____

5. Dorothy, Toto, and their friends follow the _____

6. Dorothy tries to find _____

7. The Wizard turns out to be _____

8. A scary person in the story is _____

9. The wicked witch is killed by _____

10. The hot air balloon leaves without _____

11. Dorothy uses her magic shoes to _____

Answers will vary.

Page 30

Statements and Questions

Statements are sentences that tell about something. Statements begin with a capital letter and end with a period. **Questions** are sentences that ask about something. Questions begin with a capital letter and end with a question mark.

Directions: Rewrite the sentences using capital letters and either a period or a question mark.

Example: walruses live in the Arctic

   Walruses live in the Arctic.

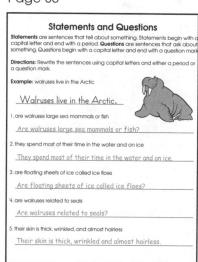

1. are walruses large sea mammals or fish

   Are walruses large sea mammals or fish?

2. they spend most of their time in the water and on ice

   They spend most of their time in the water and on ice.

3. are floating sheets of ice called ice floes

   Are floating sheets of ice called ice floes?

4. are walruses related to seals

   Are walruses related to seals?

5. their skin is thick, wrinkled, and almost hairless

   Their skin is thick, wrinkled and almost hairless.

Page 31

Commands

Commands tell someone to do something. **Example:** "Be careful." It can also be written as "Be careful!" if it tells a strong feeling.

Directions: Put a period at the end of the command sentences. Use an exclamation point if the sentence tells a strong feeling. Write your own commands on the lines below.

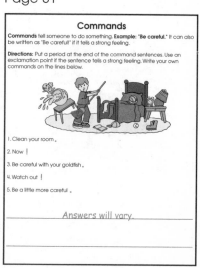

1. Clean your room .

2. Now !

3. Be careful with your goldfish .

4. Watch out !

5. Be a little more careful .

   Answers will vary.

Page 32

Questions

Questions are sentences that ask something. They begin with a capital letter and end with a question mark.

Directions: Write the questions on the lines below. Begin each sentence with a capital letter and end it with a question mark.

1. will you be my friend
   Will you be my friend?

2. what is your name
   What is your name?

3. are you eight years old
   Are you eight years old?

4. do you like rainbows
   Do you like rainbows?

Page 33

Main Idea

Directions: Circle the sentence in each paragraph that does not support the main idea.

The school picnic was so much fun! When we arrived, we each made a name tag. Then we signed up for the contests we wanted to enter. My best friend was my partner for every contest. The hen laid so many eggs that I needed a basket to carry them. All that exercise made us very hungry. We were glad to see those tables full of food.

The storm howled outside, so we stayed in for an evening of fun. The colorful rainbow stretched across the sky. The dining room table was stacked with games and puzzles. The delightful smell of popcorn led us into the kitchen where Dad led a parade around the kitchen table. Then we carried our bowls of popcorn into the dining room. We laughed so hard and ate so much, we didn't care who won the games. It was a great evening!

The city championship game would be played on Saturday at Brookside Park. Coach Metzger called an extra practice Friday evening. He said he knew we were good, because we had made it this far. He didn't want us to get nervous and forget everything we knew. School starts on Monday, but I'm not ready to go back yet. After working on some drills, Coach told us to relax, get lots of rest, and come back ready to play.

Page 34

Main Idea: Chewing Gum

Directions: Read about chewing gum, then answer the questions.

Thomas Adams was an American inventor. In 1870, he was looking for a substitute for rubber. He was working with **chicle** (chick-ul), a substance that comes from a certain kind of tree in Mexico. Years ago, Mexicans chewed chicle. Thomas Adams decided to try it for himself. He liked it so much he started selling it. Twenty years later, he owned a large factory that produced chewing gum.

1. Who was the American inventor who started selling chewing gum? _Thomas Adams_

2. What was he hoping to invent? _a substitute for rubber_

3. When did he invent chewing gum? _in 1870_

4. Where does the chicle come from? _a tree in Mexico_

5. Why did Thomas Adams start selling chewing gum? _He liked it so much._

6. How long was it until Adams owned a large factory that produced chewing gum? _20 years_

Page 35

Main Idea: Clay Homes

Directions: Read about adobe houses, then answer the questions.

Pueblo Native Americans live in houses made of clay. They are called **adobe** (ah-doe-bee) **houses.** Adobe is a yellow-colored clay that comes from the ground. The hot sun in New Mexico and Arizona helps dry the clay to make strong bricks. The Pueblos have used adobe to build their homes for many years.

Pueblos use adobe for other purposes, too. The women in the tribes make beautiful pottery out of adobe. While the clay is still damp, they form it into shapes. After they have made the bowls and other containers, they paint them with lovely designs.

1. What is the subject of this story? _adobe_

2. Who uses clay to make their houses? _Pueblo Native Americans_

3. How long have they been building adobe houses? _many years_

4. Why do adobe bricks need to be dried? _to make the clay bricks strong_

5. How do the Pueblos make pottery from adobe? _by forming damp clay_

Page 36

Noting Details

Directions: Read the story. Then answer the questions.

The giant panda is much smaller than a brown bear or a polar bear. In fact, a horse weighs about four times as much as a giant panda. So why is it called "giant"? It is giant next to another kind of panda called the red panda.

The red panda also lives in China. The red panda is about the size of a fox. It has a long, fluffy, striped tail and beautiful reddish fur. It looks very much like a raccoon.

Many people think the giant pandas are bears. They look like bears. Even the word panda is Chinese for "white bear." But because of its relationship to the red panda, many scientists now believe that the panda is really more like a raccoon!

1. Why is the giant panda called "giant"?
   It is larger than the red panda.

2. Where does the red panda live?
   in China

3. How big is the red panda?
   about the size of a fox

4. What animal does the red panda look like?
   a raccoon

5. What does the word panda mean?
   "white bear"

Page 37

Recalling Details: Nikki's Pets

Directions: Read about Nikki's pets, then answer the questions.

Nikki has two cats, Tiger and Sniffer, and two dogs, Spot and Wiggles. Tiger is an orange striped cat who likes to sleep under a big tree and pretend she is a real tiger. Sniffer is a gray cat who likes to sniff the flowers in Nikki's garden. Spot is a Dalmatian with many black spots. Wiggles is a big furry brown dog who wiggles all over when he is happy.

1. Which dog is brown and furry? _Wiggles_

2. What color is Tiger? _orange with stripes_

3. What kind of dog is Spot? _Dalmation_

4. Which cat likes to sniff flowers? _Sniffer_

5. Where does Tiger like to sleep? _under a big tree_

6. Who wiggles all over when he is happy? _Wiggles_

Page 38

Reading for Details

Directions: Read the story about bike safety. Answer the questions below the story.

Mike has a red bike. He likes his bike. Mike wears a helmet. Mike wears knee pads and elbow pads. They keep him safe. Mike stops at signs. Mike looks both ways. Mike is safe on his bike.

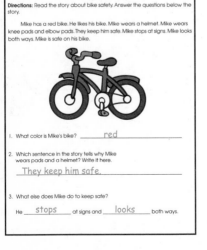

1. What color is Mike's bike? _red_

2. Which sentence in the story tells why Mike wears pads and a helmet? Write it here.
   They keep him safe.

3. What else does Mike do to keep safe?
   He _stops_ at signs and _looks_ both ways.

Page 39

Following Directions

Directions: Read the story. Answer the questions. Try the recipe.

Cows Give Us Milk

Cows live on a farm. The farmer milks the cow to get milk. Many things are made from milk. We make ice cream, sour cream, cottage cheese, and butter from milk. Butter is fun to make! You can learn to make your own butter. First, you need cream. Put the cream in a jar and shake it. Then you need to pour off the liquid. Next, you put the butter in a bowl. Add a little salt and stir! Finally, spread it on crackers and eat!

1. What animal gives us milk? _cow_

2. What 4 things are made from milk?
   ice cream _sour cream_ _cottage cheese_ _butter_

3. What did the story teach you to make? _butter_

4. Put the steps in order. Place 1, 2, 3, or 4 by the sentence.
   _4_ Spread the butter on crackers and eat!
   _2_ Shake cream in a jar.
   _1_ Start with cream.
   _3_ Add salt to the butter.

Page 40

Sequencing: 1, 2, 3, 4!

Directions: Write numbers by each sentence to show the order of the story.

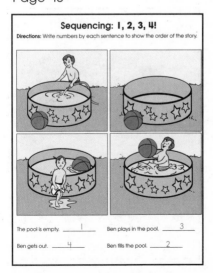

The pool is empty. _1_   Ben plays in the pool. _3_

Ben gets out. _4_   Ben fills the pool. _2_

Summer Link Reading Grade 3

Page 41

Sequencing: Yo-Yo Trick

Directions: Read about the yo-yo trick.

Wind up the yo-yo string. Hold the yo-yo in your hand. Now, hold your palm up. Throw the yo-yo downward on the string. Hold your palm down. Now, swing the yo-yo forward. Make it "walk." This yo-yo trick is called "walk the dog."

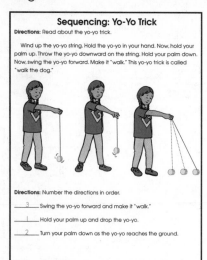

Directions: Number the directions in order.

3 Swing the yo-yo forward and make it "walk."

1 Hold your palm up and drop the yo-yo.

2 Turn your palm down as the yo-yo reaches the ground.

Page 42

Sequencing/Predicting: A Game for Cats

Directions: Read about what cats like. Then follow the instructions.

Cats like to play with paper bags. Pull a paper bag open. Take everything out. Now, lay it on its side.

1. Write 1, 2, and 3 to put the pictures in order.
2. In box 4, draw what you think the cat will do.

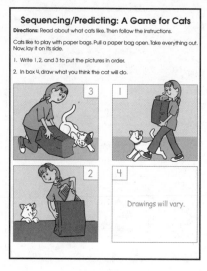

Drawings will vary.

Page 43

Sequencing: Story Events

Mari was sick yesterday.

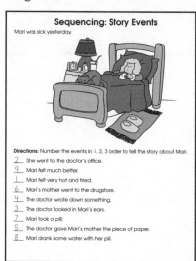

Directions: Number the events in 1, 2, 3 order to tell the story about Mari.

2 She went to the doctor's office.

9 Mari felt much better.

1 Mari felt very hot and tired.

6 Mari's mother went to the drugstore.

4 The doctor wrote down something.

3 The doctor looked in Mari's ears.

7 Mari took a pill.

5 The doctor gave Mari's mother the piece of paper.

8 Mari drank some water with her pill.

Page 44

Sequencing: Why Does It Rain?

Directions: Read about rain, then follow the instructions.

Clouds are made up of little drops of ice and water. They push and bang into each other. Then they join together to make bigger drops and begin to fall. More raindrops cling to them. They become heavy and fall quickly to the ground.

Write **first, second, third, fourth,** and **fifth** to put the events in order.

fourth More raindrops cling to them.

first Clouds are made up of little drops of ice and water.

third They join together and make bigger drops that begin to fall.

second The drops of ice and water bang into each other.

fifth The drops become heavy and fall quickly to the ground.

Page 46

Sequencing: A Story

The Crow and the Robin

The robin flew to another tree and kept on singing, but the crow sat still and made himself very unhappy. "The wind is so cold," he said. "It always blows the wrong way for me."

Very soon the sun came out, warm and bright, and the clouds went away, but the crow was as cross as ever.

The grass began to spring up in the meadows. Green leaves and flowers were seen in the woods. Birds and bees flew here and there in the glad sunshine. The crow sat and croaked on the branch of the old oak tree.

"It is always too warm or too cold," said he. "To be sure, it is a little pleasant just now, but I know that the sun will soon shine warm enough to burn me up. Then before night, it will be colder than ever. I do not see how anyone can sing at such a time as this."

Just then the robin came back to the tree with a straw in her mouth for her nest. "Well, my friend," asked she, "where is your snow?"

"Don't talk about that," croaked the crow. "It will snow all the harder for this sunshine."

"And snow or shine," said the robin, "you will keep on croaking. For my part, I shall always look on the bright side of things and have a song for every day in the year."

Which will you be like—the crow or the robin? Answers will vary.

Page 47

Sequencing: The Story

These sentences retell the story of "The Crow and the Robin" but are out of order.

Directions: Write the numbers 1 through 10 on the lines to show the correct sequence. The first one has been done for you.

7 Although the sun came out and the clouds went away, the crow was still as cross as ever.

10 "I shall always . . . have a song for every day in the year," said the robin.

1 The crow sat on the branch of an old oak tree and could only say, "Croak! Croak!"

6 "This wind is so cold. It always blows the wrong way," the crow said.

4 The crow said, "It is going to snow."

2 The robin said good morning to the crow.

5 The crow told the robin that he thought she was very foolish.

8 The grass began to spring up in the meadows.

3 The robin was jumping from branch to branch as she talked to the crow.

9 The robin came back with straw in her mouth for her nest.

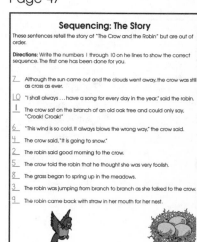

Page 48

Tracking: Alternate Paths

Look at Spotty Dog's home. Look at the paths he takes to the oven and the back door. The numbers by each path show how many steps Spotty must take to get there.

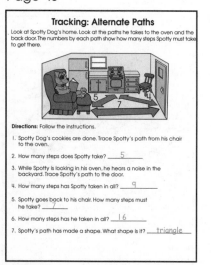

Directions: Follow the instructions.

1. Spotty Dog's cookies are done. Trace Spotty's path from his chair to the oven.
2. How many steps does Spotty take? 5
3. While Spotty is looking in his oven, he hears a noise in the backyard. Trace Spotty's path to the door.
4. How many steps has Spotty taken in all? 9
5. Spotty goes back to his chair. How many steps must he take? 7
6. How many steps has he taken in all? 16
7. Spotty's path has made a shape. What shape is it? triangle

Page 49

Same/Different: Venn Diagram

A **Venn diagram** is a diagram that shows how two things are the same and different.

Directions: Choose two outdoor sports. Then follow the instructions to complete the Venn diagram.

1. Write the first sport name under the first circle. Write some words that describe the sport. Write them in the first circle.
2. Write the second sport name under the second circle. Write some words that describe the sport. Write them in the circle.
3. Where the 2 circles overlap, write some words that describe both sports.

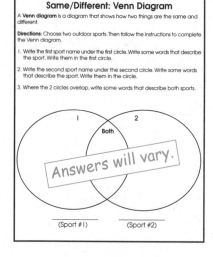

Answers will vary.

(Sport #1)   (Sport #2)

Page 50

Same/Different: Marvin and Mugsy

Directions: Read about Marvin and Mugsy. Then complete the Venn diagram, telling how they are the same and different.

Marcy has two dogs, Marvin and Mugsy. Marvin is a black-and-white spotted Dalmatian. Marvin likes to run after balls in the backyard. His favorite food is Canine Crunchy Crunch. Marcy likes to take Marvin for walks, because dogs need exercise. Marvin loves to sleep in his doghouse. Mugsy is a big furry brown dog, who wiggles when she is happy. Since she is big, she needs lots of exercise. So Marcy takes her for walks in the park. Her favorite food is Canine Crunchy Crunch. Mugsy likes to sleep on Marcy's bed.

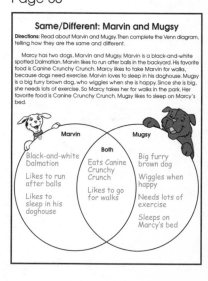

Marvin
Black-and-white Dalmation
Likes to run after balls
Likes to sleep in his doghouse

Both
Eats Canine Crunchy Crunch
Likes to go for walks

Mugsy
Big furry brown dog
Wiggles when happy
Needs lots of exercise
Sleeps on Marcy's bed

Page 51

Same/Different: Ann and Lee Have Fun

Directions: Read about Ann and Lee. Then write how they are the same and different in the Venn diagram.

Ann and Lee like to play ball. They like to jump rope. Lee likes to play a card game called "Old Maid." Ann likes to play a card game called "Go Fish." What do you do to have fun?

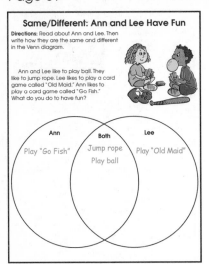

Ann — Play "Go Fish"

Both — Jump rope / Play ball

Lee — Play "Old Maid"

Page 52

Classifying

Directions: Read each animal story. Then look at the fun facts. Write an **H** for horse, **P** for panda, or **D** for dog next to each fact.

Horses
Horses are fun to ride. You can ride them in the woods or in fields. Horses usually have pretty names. Sometimes, if they are golden, they are called Amber. Horses swish their tails when it is hot. That keeps the flies away from them.

Pandas
Pandas are from China. They like to climb trees. They scratch bark to write messages to their friends in the trees. When pandas get hungry, they gnaw on bamboo shoots.

Dogs
Dogs are good pets. People often call them by names like Spot or Fido. Sometimes they are named after their looks. For example, a brown dog is sometimes named Brownie. Some people have special, small doors for their dogs to use.

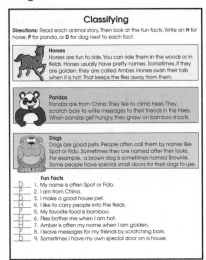

Fun Facts
D 1. My name is often Spot or Fido.
P 2. I am from China.
D 3. I make a good house pet.
H 4. I like to carry people into the fields.
P 5. My favorite food is bamboo.
H 6. Flies bother me when I am hot.
H 7. Amber is often my name when I am golden.
P 8. I leave messages for my friends by scratching bark.
D 9. Sometimes I have my own special door on a house.

Page 53

Classifying

Classifying is putting similar things into groups.

Directions: Write each word from the word box on the correct line.

baby	donkey	whale	family	fox
uncle	goose	grandfather	kangaroo	policeman

people
baby
family
grandfather
policeman
uncle

animal
goose
whale
fox
kangaroo
donkey

Page 54

Classifying: Watch Out for Poison Ivy!

Poison ivy is not safe. If you touch it, it can make your skin red and itchy. It can hurt. It grows on the ground. It has three leaves. It can be green or red. Watch out. Jay! There is poison ivy in these woods.

Directions: Color the poison ivy leaves red. Then color the "safe" leaves other colors.

Page 55

Comprehension: Sea Horses Look Strange!

Directions: Read about sea horses. Then answer the questions.

Sea horses are fish, not horses. A sea horse's head looks like a horse's head. It has a tail like a monkey's tail. A sea horse looks very strange!

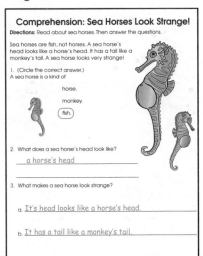

1. (Circle the correct answer.)
A sea horse is a kind of
horse.
monkey.
(fish.)

2. What does a sea horse's head look like?
a horse's head

3. What makes a sea horse look strange?
a. It's head looks like a horse's head.
b. It has a tail like a monkey's tail.

Page 56

Comprehension: How to Stop a Dog Fight

Directions: Read about how to stop a dog fight. Then answer the questions.

Sometimes dogs fight. They bark loudly. They may bite. Do not try to pull apart fighting dogs. Turn on a hose and spray them with water. This will stop the fight.

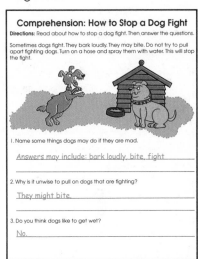

1. Name some things dogs may do if they are mad.
Answers may include: bark loudly, bite, fight

2. Why is it unwise to pull on dogs that are fighting?
They might bite.

3. Do you think dogs like to get wet?
No.

Page 57

Comprehension: A Winter Story

Directions: Read about winter. Then follow the instructions.

It is cold in winter. Snow falls. Water freezes. Most kids like to play outdoors. Some kids make a snowman. Some kids skate. What do you do in winter?

1. Circle the main idea:
Snow falls in winter.
(In winter, there are many things to do outside.)

2. Write two things about winter weather.
1) _____
2) _____

3. Write what you like to do in winter.

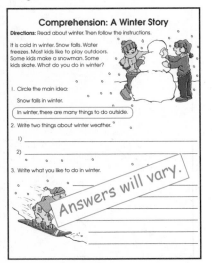

Answers will vary.

Page 58

Comprehension: More About Snakes!

Directions: Read more about snakes. Then follow the instructions.

Unlike people, snakes have cold blood. They like to be warm. They hunt for food when it is warm. They lie in the sun. When it is cold, snakes curl up into a ball.

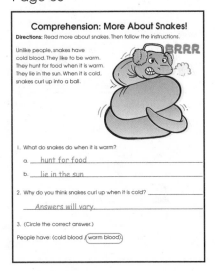

1. What do snakes do when it is warm?
a. hunt for food
b. lie in the sun

2. Why do you think snakes curl up when it is cold? _____
Answers will vary.

3. (Circle the correct answer.)
People have: (cold blood (warm blood))

Page 59

Comprehension: Ant Farms

Directions: Read about ant farms. Then answer the questions.

Ant farms are sold at toy stores and pet stores. Ant farms come in a flat frame. The frame has glass on each side. Inside the glass is sand. The ants live in the sand.

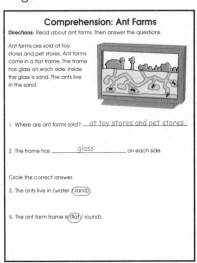

1. Where are ant farms sold? at toy stores and pet stores

2. The frame has glass on each side.

Circle the correct answer.
3. The ants live in (water (sand))

4. The ant farm frame is ((flat) round).

Summer Link Reading Grade 3

Page 60

Comprehension: Sharks Are Fish, Too!

Directions: Read the story. Then follow the instructions.

Angela learned a lot about sharks when her class visited the city aquarium. She learned that sharks are fish. Some sharks are as big as an elephant, and some can fit into a small paper bag. Sharks have no bones. They have hundreds of teeth, and when they lose them, they grow new ones. They eat animals of any kind. Whale sharks are the largest of all fish.

1. Circle the main idea:

   (Angela learned a lot about sharks at the aquarium.)

   Some sharks are as big as elephants.

2. When sharks lose teeth, they ___grow new ones___

3. ___Whale sharks___ are the largest of all fish.

4. Sharks have bones. (Circle the answer.)

   Yes   (No)

Page 61

Comprehension: Outdoor/Indoor Games

Directions: Read the story. Then answer the questions.

Derrick likes to play outdoor and indoor games. His favorite outdoor game is baseball because he likes to hit the ball with the bat and run around the bases. He plays this game in the park with the neighborhood kids.

When it rains, he plays checkers with Lorenzo on the dining-room table in his apartment. He likes the game, because he has to use his brain to think about his next move, and the rules are easy to follow.

1. What is your favorite outdoor game? _____

2. Why do you like this game? _____

3. Where is this game played? _____

4. What is you _____

5. Why do yo _____

6. Where is this game played? _____

Answers will vary.

Page 62

Comprehension: Early Trucks

What would we do without trucks? Your family may not own a truck, but everyone depends on trucks. Trucks bring our food to stores. Trucks deliver our furniture. Trucks carry new clothes to shopping centers. The goods of the world move on trucks.

Trucks are harder to make than cars. They must be sturdy. They carry heavy loads. They cannot break down.

The first trucks were on the road in 1900. Like trains, they were powered by steam engines. They did not use gasoline. The first trucks did not have heavy wheels. Their engines often broke down.

Trucks changed when the U.S. entered World War I in 1917. Big, heavy tires were put on trucks. Gasoline engines were used. Trucks used in war had to be sturdy. Lives were at stake!

Directions: Answer these questions about the first trucks.

1. What powered the first trucks?

   ___steam engines___

2. When did early trucks begin using gasoline engines?

   ___in 1917 during World War I___

3. How do trucks serve us?

   ___They deliver food, furniture and other goods of___
   ___the world.___

4. Why did trucks used in war have to be sturdy?

   ___because lives were at stake___

Page 63

Predicting: A Rainy Game

Predicting is telling what is likely to happen based on the facts.

Directions: Read the story. Then check each sentence below that tells how the story could end.

One cloudy day, Juan and his baseball team, the Bears, played the Crocodiles. It was the last half of the fifth inning, and it started to rain. The coaches and umpires had to decide what to do.

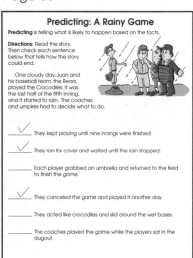

___ They kept playing until nine innings were finished.

✓ They ran for cover and waited until the rain stopped.

___ Each player grabbed an umbrella and returned to the field to finish the game.

✓ They canceled the game and played it another day.

___ They acted like crocodiles and slid around the wet bases.

___ The coaches played the game while the players sat in the dugout.

Page 64

Predicting Outcome

Directions: Read the story. Complete the story in the last box.

1. "Look at that elephant! He sure is big!"

3. "Stop, Amy! Look at that sign!"

2. "I'm hungry." "I bet that elephant is, too."

4. ___Answers will vary.___

Drawings will vary.

Page 65

Fact and Opinion

A **fact** is something that can be proven. An **opinion** is a feeling or belief about something and cannot be proven.

Directions: Read these sentences about different games. Then write **F** next to each fact and **O** next to each opinion.

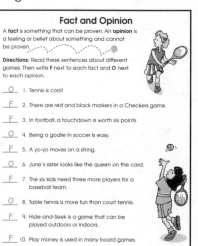

O   1. Tennis is cool!

F   2. There are red and black markers in a Checkers game.

F   3. In football, a touchdown is worth six points.

O   4. Being a goalie in soccer is easy.

F   5. A yo-yo moves on a string.

O   6. June's sister looks like the queen on the card.

F   7. The six kids need three more players for a baseball team.

O   8. Table tennis is more fun than court tennis.

F   9. Hide-and-Seek is a game that can be played outdoors or indoors.

F   10. Play money is used in many board games.

Page 66

Fact and Opinion

Directions: Read the story. Then follow the instructions.

Tashi's family likes to go to the zoo. Her favorite animals are all the different kinds of birds. Tashi likes birds because they can fly, they have colorful feathers, and they make funny noises.

Write **F** next to each fact and **O** next to each opinion.

F   1. Birds have two feet.

F   2. All birds lay eggs.

O   3. Parrots are too noisy.

F   4. All birds have feathers and wings.

O   5. It would be great to be a bird and fly south for the winter.

F   6. Birds have hard beaks or bills instead of teeth.

O   7. Pigeons are fun to watch.

F   8. Some birds cannot fly.

O   9. Parakeets make good pets.

F   10. A penguin is a bird.

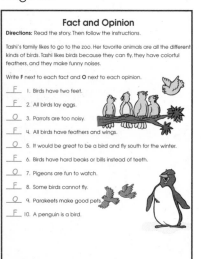

Page 67

Making Inferences

Directions: Read the story. Then answer the questions.

Mrs. Sweet looked forward to a visit from her niece, Candy. In the morning, she cleaned her house. She also baked a cherry pie. An hour before Candy was to arrive, the phone rang. Mrs. Sweet said, "I understand." When she hung up the phone, she looked very sad.

1. Who do you think called Mrs. Sweet? *Answers may include:*

   ___Candy called Mrs. Sweet.___

2. How do you know that?

   ___Mrs. Sweet probably said, "I understand," when Candy___
   ___said she wouldn't visit today.___

3. Why is Mrs. Sweet sad?

   ___Her niece, Candy, probably can't come visit today.___

Page 68

Making Inferences

Juniper has three problems to solve. She needs your help.

Directions: Read each problem. Write what you think she should do.

1. Juniper is watching her favorite TV show when the power goes out.

   _____

2. Juniper is riding her bike to school _____

3. Juniper loses her father while shopping in the supermarket.

   _____

Answers will vary.

Page 69

Making Inferences

Help make a "doggie pizza" for Spotty Dog. The steps to follow are all mixed-up. Three of the steps are not needed.

Directions: Number the steps in order from 1 to 7. Draw a dog bone by the 3 steps that are not needed.

- 3 Place the dough on a round pan.
- 5 Cover the top with cheese.
- 🦴 Take a nap.
- 1 Make the pizza dough.
- 🦴 Run out the door.
- 7 Bake it in a hot oven.
- 2 Roll the dough out flat.
- 🦴 Play ball with Spotty.
- 4 Spread the sauce on the dough.
- 6 Sprinkle bits of dog biscuits on top.

Directions: Draw Spotty Dog's pizza in the box.

Drawings will vary.

Page 70

Making Deductions

Dad is cooking dinner tonight. You can find out what day of the week it is.

Directions: Read the clues. Complete the menu. Answer the question.

Menu

- Monday _pizza_
- Tuesday _chicken_
- Wednesday _corn-on-the-cob_
- Thursday _meat pie_
- Friday _hot dogs_
- Saturday _fish_
- Sunday _cheese rolls_

1. Mom fixed pizza on Monday.
2. Dad fixed cheese rolls the day before that.
3. Tess made meat pie three days after Mom fixed pizza.
4. Tom fixed corn-on-the-cob the day before Tess made meat pie.
5. Mom fixed hot dogs the day after Tess made meat pie.
6. Tess cooked fish the day before Dad fixed cheese rolls.
7. Dad is making chicken today. What day is it? _Tuesday_

Page 71

Drawing Conclusions: Mrs. Posy's Roses

Directions: Read more about Mrs. Posy, then answer the questions.

Mrs. Posy is working in her rose garden. She is trimming the branches so that the plants will grow better. Mrs. Posy is careful, because rose bushes have thorns on them. "Hello, Mrs. Posy!" calls Ann as she rides her bicycle down the street. "Hi, Ann!" replies Mrs. Posy. Then she yells, "Ouch!" She runs inside the house and stays there for a few minutes. When Mrs. Posy comes back outside, she has a bandage on one finger.

1. Why is Mrs. Posy careful when she works with rose bushes?
   They have thorns on them.

2. Why does Mrs. Posy look up from her work? _Ann calls to her so she looks up._

3. Why did Mrs. Posy yell, "Ouch!"? _She hurt her finger on a thorn._

4. Why did Mrs. Posy run into the house? _She went to get a bandage for her finger._

Page 72

Drawing Conclusions: Eskimos

Directions: Read about the traditional lives of Eskimos, then answer the questions.

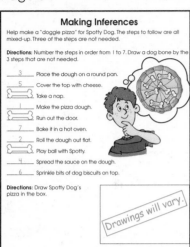

Eskimos live in Alaska. A long time ago, Eskimos lived in houses made of snow, dirt, or animal skins. They moved around from place to place. The Eskimos hunted and fished. They often ate raw meat because they had no way to cook it. When they ate meat raw, they liked it dried or frozen. Eskimos used animal skins for their clothes. They used fat from whales, seals, and other animals to heat their houses.

1. Why did the Eskimos make houses out of snow? _They had a lot of snow they could use and very little wood._

2. How did they prepare their raw meat? _They dried or froze their meat._

3. How might they use animal fat to heat their houses? _Answers will vary._

Page 73

Review

Directions: Read the story. Then answer the questions.

Randa, Emily, Ali, Dave, Liesl, and Deana all love to read. Every Tuesday, they all go to the library together and pick out their favorite books. Randa likes books about fish. Emily likes books about sports and athletes. Ali likes books about art. Dave likes books about wild animals. Liesl likes books with riddles and puzzles. Deanna likes books about cats and dogs.

1. Circle the main idea:

   Randa, Emily, Ali, Dave, Liesl, and Deana are good friends.

   (Randa, Emily, Ali, Dave, Liesl, and Deana all like books.)

2. Who do you think might grow up to be an artist?
   Ali

3. Who do you think might grow up to be an oceanographer (someone who studies the ocean)?
   Randa

4. Who do you think might grow up to be a veterinarian (an animal doctor)?
   Deanna

5. Who do you think might grow up to be a zookeeper (someone who cares for zoo animals)?
   Dave

Page 74

Cause and Effect

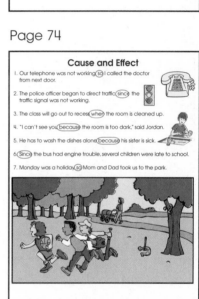

1. Our telephone was not working (so) I called the doctor from next door.

2. The police officer began to direct traffic (since) the traffic signal was not working.

3. The class will go out to recess (when) the room is cleaned up.

4. "I can't see you (because) the room is too dark," said Jordan.

5. He has to wash the dishes alone (because) his sister is sick.

6. (Since) the bus had engine trouble, several children were late to school.

7. Monday was a holiday (so) Mom and Dad took us to the park.

Page 75

Compare and Contrast

To **compare** means to discuss how things are similar. To **contrast** means to discuss how things are different.

Directions: Compare and contrast how people grow gardens. Write at least two answers for each question.

Many people in the country have large gardens. They have a lot of space, so they can plant many kinds of vegetables and flowers. Since the gardens are usually quite large, they use a wheelbarrow to carry the tools they need. Sometimes they even have to carry water or use a garden hose.

People who live in the city do not always have enough room for a garden. Many people in big cities live in apartment buildings. They can put in a window box or use part of their balcony space to grow things. Most of the time, the only garden tools they need are a hand trowel to loosen the dirt and a watering can to make sure the plant gets enough water.

1. Compare gardening in the country with gardening in the city.
   Both can plant vegetables and flowers. They both have to use tools and water.

2. Contrast gardening in the country with gardening in the city.
   City gardeners usually have smaller gardens and do not need as many tools as the country gardeners.

Page 76

Fiction and Nonfiction

Fiction writing is a story that has been invented. The story might be about things that could really happen (realistic) or about things that couldn't possibly happen (fantasy). **Nonfiction** writing is based on facts. It usually gives information about people, places, or things. A person can often tell while reading whether a story or book is fiction or nonfiction.

Directions: Read the paragraphs below and on page 77. Determine whether each paragraph is fiction or nonfiction. Circle the letter **F** for fiction or the letter **N** for nonfiction.

"Do not be afraid, little flowers," said the oak. "Close your yellow eyes in sleep and trust in me. You have made me glad many a time with your sweetness. Now, I will take care that the winter shall do you no harm. (F) N

The whole team watched as the ball soared over the outfield fence. The game was over! It was hard to walk off the field and face parents, friends, and each other. It had been a long season. Now, they would have to settle for second place. (F) N

Be careful when you remove the dish from the microwave. It will be very hot, so take care not to get burned by the dish or the hot steam. If time permits, leave the dish in the microwave for 2 or 3 minutes to avoid getting burned. It is a good idea to use a potholder, too. F (N)

Page 77

Fiction and Nonfiction

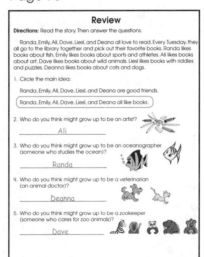

Megan and Mariah skipped out to the playground at recess. Today, it was Mariah's turn to choose what they would do first. To Megan's surprise, Mariah asked, "What do you want to do, Megan? I'm going to let you pick since it's your birthday!" (F) N

It is easy to tell an insect from a spider. An insect has three body parts and six legs. A spider has eight legs and no wings. Of course, if you see the creature spinning a web, you will know what it is. An insect wouldn't want to get too close to the web or it would be stuck. It might become dinner! F (N)

My name is Lee Chang, and I live in a country that you call China. My home is on the other side of the world from yours. When the sun is rising in my country, it is setting in yours. When it is day at your home, it is night at mine. F (N)

Henry washed the dog's foot in cold water from the brook. The dog lay very still, for he knew that the boy was trying to help him. (F) N

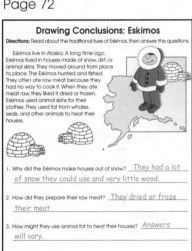

Summer Link Reading Grade 3

Page 78

Fantasy and Reality

Something that is **real** could actually happen. Something that is **fantasy** is not real. It could not happen.

Examples: **Real:** Dogs can bark.
Fantasy: Dogs can fly.

Directions: Look at the sentences below. Write **real** or **fantasy** next to each sentence.

1. My cat can talk to me. _fantasy_
2. Witches ride brooms and cast spells. _fantasy_
3. Dad can mow the lawn. _real_
4. I ride a magic carpet to school. _fantasy_
5. I have a man-eating tree. _fantasy_
6. My sandbox has toys in it. _real_
7. Mom can bake chocolate chip cookies. _real_
8. Mark's garden has tomatoes and corn in it. _real_
9. Jack grows candy and ice cream in his garden. _fantasy_
10. I make my bed everyday. _real_

Write your own **real** sentence. _Answers will vary._

Write your own **fantasy** sentence. _Answers will vary._

Page 79

Learning Dictionary Skills

A dictionary is a book that gives the meaning of words. It also tells how words sound. Words in a dictionary are in alphabetical order. That makes them easier to find. A picture dictionary lists a word, a picture of the word, and its meaning.

Directions: Look at this page from a picture dictionary, then answer the questions.

baby — A very young child.
band — A group of people who play music.
bank — A place where money is kept.
bark — The sound a dog makes.
berry — A small, juicy fruit.
board — A flat piece of wood.

1. What is a small, juicy fruit? _berry_
2. What is a group of people who play music? _band_
3. What is the name for a very young child? _baby_
4. What is a flat piece of wood called? _board_

Page 80

Making Inferences: Dictionary Mystery

Directions: Below are six dictionary entries with pronunciations and definitions. The only things missing are the entry words. Write the correct entry words. Be sure to spell each word correctly.

Entry word: _rose_
(rōz)
A flower that grows on bushes and vines.

Entry word: _rabbit_
(ra bet)
A small animal that has long ears.

Entry word: _fox_
(fäks)
A wild animal that lives in the woods.

Entry word: _piano_
(pē an ō)
A musical instrument that has many keys.

Entry word: _lake_
(lāk)
A body of water that is surrounded by land.

Entry word: _baseball_
(bās bol)
A game played with a bat and a ball.

Directions: Now write the entry words in alphabetical order.

1. _baseball_
2. _fox_
3. _lake_
4. _piano_
5. _rabbit_
6. _rose_

Page 81

Reading for Information: Newspapers

A newspaper has many parts. Some of the parts of a newspaper are:

* banner — the name of the paper
* lead story — the top news item
* caption — sentences under the picture which give information about the picture
* sports — scores and information on current sports events
* comics — drawings that tell funny stories
* editorial — an article by the editor expressing an opinion about something
* ads — paid advertisements
* weather — information about the weather
* advice column — letters from readers asking for help with a problem
* movie guides — a list of movies and movie times
* obituary — information about people who have died

Directions: Match the newspaper sections below with their definitions.

banner — an article by the editor
lead story — sentences under pictures
caption — movies and movie times
editorial — the name of the paper
movies — information about people who have died
obituary — the top news item

Page 82

Library Skills: Alphabetical Order

Ms. Ling, the school librarian, needs help shelving books. Fiction titles are arranged in alphabetical order by the author's last name. Ms. Ling has done the first set for you.

_3_ Silverstein, Shel   _1_ Bridwell, Norman   _2_ Farley, Walter

Directions: Number the following groups of authors in alphabetical order.

_2_ Bernelmans, Ludwig   _4_ Perkins, Al
_4_ Stein, R.L.   _2_ Dobbs, Rose
_3_ Sawyer, Ruth   _1_ Baldwin, James
_1_ Baum, L. Frank   _3_ Kipling, Rudyard

The content of some books is also arranged alphabetically.

Directions: Circle the books that are arranged in alphabetical order.

T.V. guide   (dictionary)   (encyclopedia)   novel
almanac   science book   (Yellow Pages)   catalog

Write the books you circled in alphabetical order.

1. _dictionary_
2. _encyclopedia_
3. _Yellow Pages_

Page 83

Periodicals

Libraries also have periodicals such as magazines and newspapers. They are called **periodicals** because they are printed regularly within a set period of time. There are many kinds of magazines. Some discuss the news. Others cover fitness, cats, or other topics of special interest. Almost every city or town has a newspaper. Newspapers usually are printed daily, weekly, or even monthly. Newspapers cover what is happening in your town and in the world. They usually include sections on sports and entertainment. They present a lot of information.

Directions: Follow the instructions.

1. Choose an interesting magazine.
   What is the name of the magazine?
   List the titles of three articles in the magazine.

   Answers will vary.

2. Now, look at a newspaper.
   What is the name of the newspaper?
   The title of a newspaper story is called a headline.
   What are some of the headlines in your local newspaper?

Page 84

Reading a Schedule

Special Saturday classes are being offered to students of the county schools. They will be given the chance to choose from art, music or gymnastics classes.

Directions: Read the schedule, then answer the questions.

	Saturday, November 13	
Art	**Music**	**Gymnastics**
8:00 A.M. Watercolor—Room 350 Clay Sculpting—Room 250	Island Rhythms—Room 54 Orchestra instruments—Stage	Floor Exercises—W. Gym Parallel Bars—E. Gym
Break (10 minutes)		
10:00 A.M. Painting Stills—Room 420 Watercolor—Room 350	Percussion—Room 54 Jazz Sounds—Stage	Uneven Bars—N. Gym
Break (10 minutes)		
11:00 A.M. Oils on Canvas—Room 258 ———	Island Rhythms—Room 54 Create Your Own Music—Room 40	Uneven Bars—N. Gym Balance Beam—W. Gym

1. Where would you meet to learn about Jazz Sounds? _on the stage_
2. Could a student sign up for Watercolor and Floor Exercises? _yes_
   Explain your answer. _They are offered at different times._
3. Which music class would a creative person enjoy? _Create Your Own Music_
4. Could a person sign up for an art class at 11:00? _yes_
5. What time is the class on clay sculpting offered? _8:00 A.M._

Developmental Skills for Third–Grade Success

McGraw-Hill, the premier educational publisher PreK–12, wants to be your partner in helping you educate your child. *Summer Link Reading* was designed to help your child retain those skills learned during the past school year. With *Summer Link Reading,* your child will be ready to review and take on new material with confidence when he or she returns to school in the fall. The skills reviewed here will help your child be prepared for proficiency testing.

You can use this checklist to evaluate your child's progress. Place a check mark in the box if the appropriate skill has been mastered. If your child needs more work with a particular skill, place an "R" in the box and come back to it for review.

Language Arts Skills

☐ Recognizes uppercase letters

☐ Recognizes lowercase letters

☐ Knows difference between consonants and vowels

☐ Knows the single letter sounds

☐ Knows digraphs ch, sh, th, wh

☐ Knows consonant and vowel blends

☐ Knows beginning, ending, and middle sounds of words

☐ Recognizes compound words

☐ Discriminates between antonyms and synonyms

☐ Discriminates between homophones and other words

Recognizes parts of speech:

☐ nouns and proper nouns

☐ verbs

☐ adjectives

☐ pronouns

☐ articles

☐ Knows how to create contractions

☐ Recognizes controlled vowels: er, ar, ir, ur, or

☐ Can break words into syllables

☐ Can look up words in a dictionary

☐ Correctly writes upper- and lowercase letters

Developmental Skills for Third–Grade Success

Language Arts Skills, continued

Uses writing strategies:

- ☐ Uses knowledge of letter sounds to create words

- ☐ Copies or traces words

- ☐ Writing shows a sequence of events or clear ideas

- ☐ Ability to use rhymes

☐ Identifies types of sentences

☐ Can identify prefixes and suffixes

☐ Recognizes meaning and use of possessives

☐ Recognizes various tenses of verbs

☐ Identifies types of sentences

☐ Recognizes subject/predicate of a sentence

☐ Recognizes complete and incomplete sentences

☐ Uses correction punctuation: ., ?, !

☐ Recognizes misspelled words

Reading Skills

Uses reading strategies:

- ☐ Uses pictures to tell a story

- ☐ Follows text from left to right

- ☐ Uses story content and pattern to predict

- ☐ Uses grammar to help decipher words

- ☐ Sounds out words

☐ Can interpret characters in a story

☐ Recalls main events in a story

☐ Recalls conflict of a story

☐ Recalls setting of a story

☐ Recalls conclusion of a story

☐ Recalls or predicts a simple sequence of events

☐ Recognizes causes and effects of situations

☐ Recognizes forms of literature (poetry, nonfiction, etc.)